GIVING THOUGHT AND ACTION TO THE
TRANSFORMATIVE POWER OF GRATITUDE

THINK ABOUT Thanks

PAM AUBLE

GREATEST THANKS TO...

Reflecting on the time I spent writing this book, my family made this possible with a positive attitude, space to create and a significant final push. Thank you, Amy, for calling me out when I walk away from my core beliefs, tangled in negativity. Sometimes I wonder who is actually raising whom. Thank you, Dave, for giving me the gift of creative space and time. You trusted me when I didn't trust myself. And thanks for a perfect title! Andy, thank you for pulling my unfinished book off the shelf. You showed me the glory of the finished product.

Jacque, what a blessing for me that Andy teamed up with you. You put together a finished product that is more attractive than I dreamed ... literally.

CONTENTS

INTRODUCTION: THANK YOU

Thank you. Do we hear that so much that our ears become immune to the sentiments? Or is it that we don't hear it often enough? And forget about hearing it; how about saying it? Is there power in those words both for us and for those to whom we speak our thanks? As the words are formed in our hearts and then leave our lips, have we any notion of what transformative potential lies in feeling grateful?

Together in these pages we will explore the inherent power of thanks, in seeing cause for thanks, in saying and expressing our thanks, and going full bore into living our thanks.

When fully expressed, thanks is not simply given, as in writing a thank you card or telling someone thanks. Rather, thanks—fully expressed—is lived, and therefore alters our perspective on people, on ourselves, and on our God! From an attitude of thankfulness, we come to recognize an endless stream of cause for feeling thanks. We see it! We crave the opportunity to share our gratefulness. We say it! And then, what inspired words of gratitude gives rise to thanks-inspired action because we find mere words are insufficient. We want to give not just a thankful nod, but live a life of thankfulness. We live it! We laugh more deeply; we love less cautiously; we share more freely; we dream more intentionally; we believe more fully in the goodness of each day.

All of this is generated by thanks. It's a simple matter of first seeing a cause for gratitude, which inspires a desire to express thanks, and creates a call to live as a person of thankfulness. These pages give sincere thought to the action of thanks as I have come to understand its three-part composition: See it! Say it! Live it! And all of it has been through the lens of faith and scripture. As the Psalmist has instructed, "Oh give thanks to the Lord!" As

Jesus gave example, let us give thanks for bread, wine, fish, and being heard. As the biblical characters Jonah, Nehemiah, Paul, and Mary lived it, we too are called to live thankfully.

I have chosen to highlight my understanding of gratitude by reflecting on scripture passages and stories. Throughout this book, Bible verses will be quoted. In many cases, the reader will find it most useful to read the entire chapter from which the verses have been taken. Context is always important for fully understanding the Scripture's intention. In other words, don't take my word, adhere to the Word, as found more fully in Scripture. In fact, the portion of scripture you find printed here may only be a single verse of the larger passage to which I refer. In other words, read the whole thing so you and God can come to a clearer understanding. I do not claim to be a biblical scholar, although I have seriously considered the potential implications of the stories and verses I refer to in these pages. For me, the Bible clearly states the case for thankful living and this book explores my findings.

Stories of family, friends, and unsuspecting acquaintances are included here, too. Sometimes I changed their names, but the stories and my experiences are all real. You can now start feeling sympathy for my children, Andy and Amy, whose lives are a constant focus of my life, and therefore of my writing. By the way, they really are every bit as amazing as I make them out to be. Just ask their dad!

How I would love to hear your stories too! Please send me your reflections, reactions and experiences with thankful living. Together, we could all write a sequel, and I'll be sure to give you credit for your input. I welcome contradictory opinions too. I know that my thankfulness binge may have left me blind to other realities. Push me, challenge me, and help me grow.

And I will do the same. In this book, I hope to push and challenge the reader. Look at a few bible stories differently. Struggle with finding thanks when feeling destitute. Try a "please and thank you" prayer. Write more thank-you notes. Reflect your thankful attitude on someone needing the attention. And never overlook God's gifts, "Give thanks to the Lord, for God is good!"

PART 1
SEE IT!

SEE IT!

We watch the sky for clues about the weather. We root for hints that he might be romantically interested. We comb the want ads for a suitable job. We search for hope in troubled economic times. We look high and low for signs of spring. What results can we expect if we look as energetically for reasons to give thanks?

They're there. Every moment of each day there is reason to feel thankful. It's time to focus our gaze on all that is right and good, true and kind, worthy and enjoyable, beautiful and loving, and just and glorious. The first step to thankful living is seeing cause to be thankful, and doing so may require altering our perspective.

If I accept only blooming tulips as a sure sign of spring, I will miss a huge portion of this magnificent season. Long before the tulips arrive in Northeast Ohio, spring offers snowdrops, daffodils, and forsythia, just to name a few. We hear the return of the songbirds, peepers, and tree frogs. The days grow longer. The grass begins to green. The air warms and fresh scents bathe the nose. Baseball season begins! Often Easter is here weeks before the tulips show their colors.

If we are not intentional about looking, we miss out on valuable findings. For instance, when my son, Andy, was much younger he seemed to find money everywhere. He's the one who'd notice the quarter left in the vending machine, a dollar in a puddle and even a twenty on the fairground boulevard. Looking for coins and bills became a part of his nature. In a similar fashion, we may need to train our mind's eye to seek every possible reason for thanks.

If I only expect to find thanks inspired by gifts wrapped in pretty paper, dinner invitations, and verbal compliments, much of what could elicit my thanks will elude me. I could see occasions for thanks lurking unexpectedly in another's joy, rather than my own. Thanks could be found in an opportunity to help a portion of God's people. Given the right frame of mind, thanks may even arise out of disappointment. As we start to seriously think about thanks, we must begin with finding every possible stimulus for gratitude. Let's just see it.

1
GIFTS

Unlike a birthday party or a wedding shower, the stack under a Christmas tree or in an Easter basket, the gifts that come our way do not usually have a gift tag with our name on it. Of course we see the cause for thanks as we unwrap the presents selected especially for our special occasion, but not every gift is as easily identified. These less obvious gifts need to be named and recognized in our thankful hearts. For instance, answered prayers call out for thankful attention. Friendship, love, healing, and health are thankworthy. Finding reason to be hopeful is also reason to be thankful. And most importantly, the gift of God's Son is something we can daily unwrap, rediscover, and rejoice in for it is the ultimate gift deserving of our thanks.

WRAPPED IN PRETTY PAPER AND BOWS

"… have all the riches of assured understanding and have the knowledge of God's mystery, that is, Christ Himself… continue to live your lives in Him … just as you were taught, abounding in thanksgiving." Colossians 2:1–7

There are times when we are just too preoccupied to recognize the need to say thank you. Sometimes someone needs to point out the beautiful gift that waits right before our eyes. We need enlightenment in order to recognize the value of the gifts we have been given.

When my family and friends gathered to surprise me and celebrate my 50th birthday, it was a great party! I loved being with everyone, eating together, sharing stories, and just seeing their faces. My husband, Dave, planned a perfect event. After hours of happy partying, some folks trickled out and headed home, even as I was still busy enjoying the event. My nephew finally had to ask me, "Aren't you going to open your gifts and cards?" All that time together and I hadn't even noticed the wrapped gifts.

Certainly the gift of their presence was enough and so this may not be the best analogy, but, stay with me here. Sometimes we miss the obvious—those gifts of life that practically come wrapped in bright, pretty paper and voluptuous bows.

The gift of God's love for us can be one such gift. We sing about it, recite ritual stating it, send Christmas cards declaring it, and yet constantly stray away from the reality of it. God does love us. And there is not a single thing we can do to change that. God's love is a gift already given to us that won't be taken back. It's yours. It's mine. The life, death, and resurrection of Christ are proof of God's unconditional love given for all. And even though we know this as fact, we still forget it as the ever-present gift that it is. This is the greatest cause for thanksgiving. Period.

As Paul writes to the Colossians, he makes it clear that Christ is the gift before them. I like the way Paul describes Christ as "God's mystery," like the birthday packages I had yet to open at the end of my party. The Colossians had already received the news of Christ as Savior from another believer. Paul wrote to articulate the fact that Jesus is a great gift! He is a gift worthy of our abounding thankfulness!

Paul confesses his struggle for the people of this place. He struggles for them because he wants so much to be sure they see the gift. They must know the richness of Christ for us: Christ's life for us and Christ's death for us. And they must understand the promise of life in Christ, as His resurrection professes. Paul's words, "so that they may have all the riches of assured understanding" express to me his desire that we all come to know this present so intimately that there are no doubts still hidden in the crevices of our hearts or our minds. If we fully understand God's mysterious love for us, we will not later misunderstand due to misinformation.

Paul wrote to the early churches, coming to them when he could, and pointed out the wrapped treasures of faith, the gift of God's love through Jesus. And this gift alone is reason for our thanks. We want to thank You, Lord!

At the end of that surprise party, my nephew sat with me as I unwrapped gifts. What an unexpected joy when I opened a handmade gift from my nephew and his fiancée—a spunky little pedestal bowl, hand painted in pink and green with Polka dots! Even now, years later, whenever I see their bowl I remember that special party with so many of my favorite people. It reminds me that I am loved and fills my heart with thanks. Paul would be happy to know that I also remember and live with gratitude for God's mysterious love wrapped in the life and love of Jesus.

A WISH LIST OR A PRAYER OF THANKS?

"Devote yourselves to prayer, keeping alert in it with thanksgiving." Colossians 4:2–4

Each fall as my birthday nears, my mom wants a wish list from me. Of course, I always have one ready. Dave doesn't ask for one, but I make sure he sees my list too. I think it's good to let my family know what I want, and we have a tradition of birthday and Christmas wish lists. However, I need to carefully limit how that concept spreads into other aspects of life.

Prayer shouldn't sound or look like a birthday wish list. Prayer is God's time to make wishes known to us, something we usually call God's will. In his letter to the Colossians, Paul wants the faithful to devote themselves to prayer **and** do so with thanks. Perhaps Paul is cautioning us to avoid wish list prayers and instead take note of how well God's previous gifts have been working. Recognizing that God has been in our midst and how blessed we are can give us the courage we need to hear what God calls us to now. A prayer conversation with God could sound like this: I see where You have led me in the past. Thank you! God, where will You lead me now? Looking where I've been and what we've come through gives me the audacity and the determination to say to You, God, let's keep going Your way.

Paul was constantly in prayer, enthusiastic about all that God had done for him and prepared to serve God wherever he was needed. Paul wrote to the Colossians while imprisoned, and even there he lived his conviction to pray with thanks at all times. Even from jail he saw an opportunity for thanks and asked those praying for him to ask **not** for his release, but rather for new opportunities in sharing faith while imprisoned. He doesn't ask for the doors of his cell to be opened for him, but rather that the doors of opportunity be opened wide so he could share his faith in Christ. By living a life alert to thanksgiving, Paul came to a place of complete trust in God.

Each December, I—along with my siblings—send out a wish list for our Christmas gift exchange. My brother, Doug, often starts his wish list with words of thanks for all that the previous year has brought us. They are great words of monumental gifts, things like health, prosperity, and family. Sometimes he brings up the pointlessness of trying to buy anything for one another that could make our lives any better. We already have it all. Maybe that's Paul's point. If we start our prayers with thanks, our list of needs diminishes, and we come to God with hearts full of thanks and a spirit ready to serve. So, if you are thinking of what to get me for my birthday, don't expect me to include my wish list here. However, I'll be happy knowing that you might say a prayer for me to see what God needs from me.

COUNT YOUR BLESSINGS

Sometime in late November, the Christmas specials begin flooding the airwaves, usually starting on Thanksgiving Day. Do you have a favorite? *It's A Wonderful Life*? *Miracle on 34th Street*? *A Charlie Brown Christmas*? *A Christmas Carol*? *The Grinch*? How about *White Christmas*? That has been one of my favorites for many years. I love Danny Kaye and Vera Ellen's dancing and Bing Crosby and Rosemary Clooney's singing. It even has a love story, a happy ending, and lots of snow.

My favorite song, even more than "White Christmas" is "Count Your Blessings (Instead of Sheep)." It's one of the few songs in the whole film without a dance routine accompanying it. Betty is having a tough time falling sleep and finds comfort in the advice sung by her new friend, Bob.

"When I'm worried and I can't sleep, I count my blessings instead of sheep, and I fall asleep, counting my blessings. When my bankroll is gettin' small, I think of when I had none at all, and I fall asleep, counting my blessings."

Bob's plan is a good one, even if we're not trying to sleep. Worry has a way of sneaking into our subconscious and disrupting not only our sleeping hours, but also our waking hours. Instead of filling our heads with "what if" and "oh no," we could be focusing on "thank you" and "what a blessing." As we make our to-do list and focus on all we haven't accomplished, we could count up all we have been able to get done and all the wonderful people we've been doing it with! When feeling scared about not having enough money to buy the gifts we want, we could find thankfulness in what we can give that doesn't cost anything. Can we give our time, our support, and our love instead of another electronic gadget? During the holidays, we can thank God for snow or complain about the cold. We can thank Aunt Betty for the scarf or murmur about its hideous color. We can be glad that Bob is well enough to join us for Christmas dinner or complain about his crude jokes.

Every day and night we have the opportunity to count our blessings or curse the messy sheep.

During a recent December when it was snowing again, I had an early morning road trip planned to visit a healing friend. The night before, the snowfall had been severe and my drive home had taken over two hours instead of 45 minutes. This is simply a part of the Christmas season in Northeast Ohio. As I faced my day, I started counting blessings right away. I had a safe car with good tires. I had loved ones at both ends of my trip. The snow was covering the earth with diamond-like sparkles. My friend was healing, and the surgeons did a wonderful job. The plow trucks would still have salt in December! I made sure, however, to pack my boots, extra food, and my cell phone. Wait. Those were three more blessings to count! So many gifts, even before Christmas morning!

Fewer worries. More blessings. Thank you God.

IN THANKS WE FIND HOPE

"For in hope we were saved. Now hope that is seen is not hope. For who hopes for what is seen. But if we hope for what we do not see, we wait for it with patience." Romans 8:24–25

During the Lent season, our hearts turn to sorrow as we release the joy of Christmas and embrace the season of sacrifice. Anne Weam writes in her poetry that in this season of the church, we are no longer on a road leading to Bethlehem with angelic voices and kingly visits to celebrate birth. We are on the road to Jerusalem and its historic denial, pain, and sacrifice. As Christians, we know what's on the other side of the crucifixion, but first we must revisit the magnitude of Christ's pain.

Which brings me to thanks. How can we dwell in joyful thanksgiving in the season of Lent? Our thanks for the sacrifice Christ made for us resides deep within us, but the sorrow and introspection of Lenten meditation can lead us to a denigrating self-reflection. Some of us come to realize that had it been us in the garden we probably would have slept too. We may have grabbed the knife and swung with anger. On the road to Jerusalem, we could have been the ones asking for seats of glory and questioning Jesus' wisdom in avoiding political leadership when His victory seemed so certain. In fear for our lives, we may have sought the safety of denial too. If not 2000 years ago, today we commit acts of betrayal in a very real sense. Lenten reflection can leave us feeling repentant and distraught about who we are and how we have failed. Basking in the bright light of thankfulness, especially the thankfulness of self-appreciation, seems to be out of sync with the attitude of Lent. And yet—without a doubt—this time is significant and rich in terms of faith maturation.

For some of us in the Auble family, Lent is like a bad basketball season followed by the hope of spring and baseball. One year, we were all glad for the end of the school basketball season—it had not been a particularly victorious season. Some of our players actually digressed, losing talent that appeared to burst forth at the season's start. We lost too many close games that year, and honestly I wanted to cry after the last game's defeat. My son, a decent player, was on that team and didn't have a great season—the one he had dreamed of in the fall. He continued to work hard at all the practices and somehow kept a positive, albeit realistic, attitude throughout the season. The morning after their last loss of the season, he dressed for school in his **baseball** jersey and said, "I can't wait for baseball to start!"

His positive attitude offers a lesson of thanks and hope for a meaningful Lenten experience. Within the seasons of life that knock us down, there is strength to be captured, optimism to be gleaned, perseverance to be gathered, and renewed vision to be realized. There is a new season! Self-reflection paints a picture of who we are and makes a rough sketch of who we could become. As a clear picture of who we are comes into focus, we see not only the missed opportunities, but also personal achievements and positive qualities. That "good side" gives rise to thanks. Likewise, in the rough sketches we can rejoice in the vision of personal potential.

That sounds like a description of hope. And perhaps there are times we are only able to say thanks because we still have hope. Hope lies in the thought that a better me is always in the making. I praise God for what I dare to believe will happen, even when I cannot see evidence of it now. A song will rise in my parched throat, and it will be an uplifting hymn of thanksgiving. I will sing from the depths of a dry well simply because my hand feels the cool moisture of the well's walls and I believe that relief is on its way.

2
ENOUGH STUFF

Very little is said in the scriptures concerning thanks for things. Thankfulness is written for grace, good works, care, and safety. There are words of praise for creation and steadfast love. Thanksgiving is showered on God for harvest, for His word, and for His Son. The scriptures record no expression of thanks for a massive accumulation of material belongings. There is no verse that says, "Thank you God for all my stuff." Perhaps that is a good warning for us.

TOO MUCH STUFF

I've spent a good deal of time thinking about thanks, having too much stuff, scripture, and how the three are related. Actually, I can't really find scripture references about material belongings and saying thanks. This isn't the way I usually go about studying scripture. Generally, I read a scripture first and then reflect on it. I find that thinking about something and then finding a scripture to back up my opinions can be pretty dangerous. But, that's another thought for another day and another book. Back to thanks...

Perhaps a lesson on thanks for stuff can be gleaned from the Gospel parable that tells of a man who wanted to store his bountiful harvest in beautiful, new barns. Unfortunately, he found that he would not live long enough to enjoy his treasure (Luke 12:13–21). He had more stuff than time.

My bounty may not be in a harvest of grain, yet I may soon be in need of a new barn to store all my accumulated stuff. We have very little storage space in our home and now that we've been here for 15 years our storage deficit is getting the best of me. Closets are full. Space under the beds is filled. The attic is cramped. The items that our family needed, had to have, desired, acquired, won, bought, or received are consuming our living space. We find we have so much stuff we don't know what all we own. Some of it that we thought would bring us joy or solve our problems isn't necessary at all. We find we're not thankful for much of it.

It's an odd dance of waste where we find ourselves tripping over our own selfish feet, trying to find the rhythm of happiness we expected to feel when our wealth gave us the opportunity to buy our dreams. The problem is in what we are expecting to gain from the act of acquisition. Owning stuff, in and of itself, can't satisfy us. Being thankful for what we have is more likely to give us cause to dance. And it's so hard to dance gracefully while carrying a sack of unnecessary goods.

ENRICHED WITH ENOUGH

"And God is able to provide you with every blessing in abundance, so that always having enough of everything, you may share abundantly in every good work... You will be enriched in every way for your great generosity, which will produce thanksgiving to God through us..." II Corinthian 9:6–15

When do I know that I have enough? When I run out of closet space, does that mean I have enough clothing? When I have separate bedrooms for each family member and an extra guest room, is my house finally big enough? When the refrigerator and the extra freezer are full, can I then be assured that I have enough food? If I can pay all my bills and still have something for the savings account, then do I know that I'm making enough money? When can I be sure that I have enough?

Maybe enough can be understood from this perspective: If I share my family's dinner with a lonely neighbor and we all go to bed feeling full, I know I had enough food for that day. From that experience, I determine that I have enough to share again tomorrow. In fact, I can fill a bag with canned goods, send it with my son to school for the food drive, and not miss it. If I walk away with no new purchases from the mall and come home to find I have enough clothes to keep me warm and dry, I might realize I certainly do have enough clothes. In fact, I might even be motivated to share some of my clothing allowance with a local agency that provides kids with coats for the winter. With a new perspective, I might ascertain that my home is very large and that there's plenty of room for someone who needs a place to stay. Could it be that instead of dedicating more hours at work in hopes of making more money, I could take those hours and donate them to community service?

In his second letter to the Corinthians, Paul assures the community that God provides such abundance that they will always have enough to share. *Generosity will bring about enrichment, which will result in thanksgiving.* I wonder just what Paul meant when he wrote, "You will be **enriched** in every way for your great generosity, which will produce thanksgiving to God through us." Paul wanted to be sure that the church in Corinth kept a promise to support the Christian ministry in Jerusalem. In these verses, he urges the faithful to give generously and expect much in return, for they will be "enriched" and God will be thanked.

Enriched. Does this mean if they give, they will become rich? Is Paul teaching us that if—from faith—we share what we have, God will make sure we become wealthy? I doubt it. But, we will be enriched. This is what Paul's words say to me: When I share what I have, I come to realize I still have enough, and I am enriched. When I give more and I learn that I need less, I am enriched. When I satisfy the needs of others, I find satisfaction. Sometimes it takes the act of giving for me to realize how much I have. I give, and then I give thanks.

Jesus said the poor will always be with us, but he didn't say that we would always be poor—so be sure to have more than enough so you never run out! In fact, in His teaching about prayer, Jesus instructs us to ask for enough for today ("Give us this day our daily bread"). Enough. Just enough. Maybe if we have more than enough, we ought to share it, so someone else will have enough and will have cause for thanks. Maybe we can learn to feel blessed and be thankful because we have enough.

Apart from this, there is a prosperity gospel that preaches a message of material abundance for the faithful Christian. From this perspective, wealth is proof of one's faithful obedience to God, and there is little talk about how that wealth is to be used or shared. It's a gospel message foreign to Jesus and Paul;

a message not written in the Hebrew Scriptures either. Instead, we read verses such as these from Psalms 112:

"Wealth and riches are in their houses, and their righteousness endures forever. They rise in the darkness as a light for the upright; they are gracious, merciful, and righteous. It is well with those who deal generously and lend, who conduct their affairs with justice… They have distributed freely, they have given to the poor; their righteousness endures forever."

In my experience, I have found many people—regardless of their wealth—who are very grateful for what they have. Those same folks—again, regardless of their wealth—are extremely generous. In other words, grateful people are generous people. They are an inspiration to me, and their lifestyle is one I want to emulate. They find themselves enriched in every way, just like Paul said, and they know they have enough, more than enough, and they want to enrich others. Because they live their thanks, their actions produce more thankful hearts. And thankfulness, like their righteousness, endures forever.

MINE!

It feels good to say mine.

The pride of ownership is pervasive in our society. Satisfaction is found in wanting it, selecting it, buying it with hard-earned cash, and taking it home. Advertisements play on this love of ownership and hype up the fulfillment that comes with having something new. Something better. Something bigger. And once it's ours, we get to care for it, buy the accessories, make the right place for it, use it, and accept the additional fees and charges that may come with owning it. And why wait until we can actually afford it? Instant gratification isn't a bad thing when credit is an option. And we can enjoy it now. Right?

Being grateful for what we already have can help alleviate the temptation of owning or buying more—or better. I am thankful that my computer still works. I don't have to have more memory and a better monitor. Even after almost 15 years, our refrigerator still runs. It will do for now. A bread maker would be nice, but how often will I actually use it? And where will I store it? My cell phone isn't the latest model, but if I buy the newest version, it will be outdated again next month. These shoes still fit, although they could use a good shine. And even though that pink shirt was a good deal, I never should have bought it. I brought it home only to find I already had one in nearly the same color and style. I guess I need to be thankful for and **aware** of all I own.

In our Mayberry-style small town, we've adopted a policy of shared ownership in some cases. For example, our chainsaw is passed up and down the street after a summer storm topples trees. At three in the morning, my husband knocked on the neighbor's door to borrow their wet-dry vacuum when our basement was filling with storm water. We loan out our tire pump each spring when kids start riding bikes up and down the street again. Although each family owns a leaf rake, this fall we'll borrow more rakes so entire families can clean the yard together. We do the same with shovels in the winter. A sledge hammer, a truck, a cake pan, a toboggan sled, a playground slide, a basketball hoop, a picnic table, a fishing boat, poles, and tackle: all of these have been loaned out or shared—duplicate purchases weren't necessary. Our neighborhood even shares an in-ground pool!

Sharing is truly fun—and there's less environmental impact. Plus, there's no need for extra storage space. And it gives us more time to interact with our neighbors. And we get to say "thank you." We love it.

My mother, who lives in another town, marvels at the way our family "shops" in the neighbor's pantry. Not a week goes by that I'm not on the phone, calling around for ingredients, while stirring a pot for dinner. Other nights, I find I'm sending my kid down the street to deliver a missing ingredient to a neighbor. My mom has witnessed this miracle of sharing during various mealtime visits, wishing for the courage to do the same in her neighborhood. Yet, borrowing and sharing are acquired skills that develop over time. They come with a mutual understanding that owning everything isn't necessary. Although ownership has its pleasures, there are burdens, too: Upkeep, payments, insurance, protection, replacement, cleaning, repair, responsibility, storage, risk, damage. None of this is mentioned in those ads. And all of it takes more money, or time, or both.

Sometimes folks find pleasure in the added responsibilities. If that is the case in your situation, please be sure to give thanks for the time and money you are spending, and don't give in to complaining about it. Owning it was your choice in the first place—be glad for the privilege of having it. Every time I see a big yacht, all I can think about is the amount of time and money that it requires. Someone is working extra hours to make more money to cover the cost of upkeep, docking, and storage. They are also spending time traveling and cleaning, before they even get to spend an afternoon enjoying it. There are many who are all too happy to do so, but not me. Our little fishing boat is enough. Knowing one's limits makes it easier to deeply feel the satisfaction of ownership, and be able to live thankfully with it.

Before buying into the myth of the joy in spending and owning, take a good look at the added responsibilities and any other options. There is joy, too, in sharing, renting, borrowing, and lending. And there is pleasure found in things not owned: Read a library book. Sing along with the radio. Rent a bike for your annual cycling outing. Borrow a tent instead of buying a camper. Share stories and memories around a campfire. Listen to your son. Laugh with your dad. Play the harmonica during the power outage. Be together.

Appreciating what we already have injects satisfaction into our blood without the need for a fresh infusion of new belongings. What I mean is this: actually take inventory of what you have and give the appropriate thanks. For instance, I have a china cabinet full of antique Fiestaware. At one time, I coveted the rainbow of bright colors I remembered from my childhood visits to two grandmas' houses. Unexpectedly, I inherited a few of these dishes. Using money we were given for our wedding, my husband and I gradually added to the small set of old dishes and found new-old plates, bowls, cups and serving pieces. More were received as gifts over the years. Now, the cabinet is full of more than a hundred pieces. They are pretty valuable as antique collector's pieces, but, they are more valuable to our family because we use them! And they lose monetary value each time we chip or crack a piece. And yet, not a day goes by that I don't think of my grandmas, or give thanks for the bright colors, or remember the fun we've had adding to the collection.

We fill the dining room table with those dishes for our children's birthday parties each year. The house gets pretty crowded when all the cousins come and we sit around the spread. The brilliance of color may have been a little too dizzying one year as my niece cleared her Fiesta dish only to drop it and watch it shatter on the tile floor. She fought tears as her face turned brighter red than the plate she had dropped. Her mom was upset with her for breaking one of my precious heirloom pieces. I immediately tried to ease their fears.

For me, it was no big deal, just an accident. The plate could have been kept safely locked away in the cabinet, just a thin line of color in a stack of unused plates—but, heck, that's no fun. Instead, that plate had been present for count-less dinners, parties, and celebrations. The dinner plate had a good life and had been well-appreciated over the years.

Precious belongings can also be stored away—and forgotten. How grateful can we be for stuff we don't even remember we own? Here is a sad, but true example: While dining with acquaintances we met on a business trip, the table talk turned to pearls—precious black pearls, actually. The other women at the table told stories of their strands, their earrings, and their rings. Lisa described her gorgeous black pearl ring she seldom wore. Oh, how she loved the glisten of a black pearl and its rare beauty! However, she scarcely wore her ring be-cause she didn't have a strand of black pearls to accompany it. The tale of her woes dragged on, as her husband grew more agitated. He was seething, and ap-parently deeply hurt. Finally, he interrupted her. "Dear, I bought you a strand of black pearls for our last anniversary." I felt so sorry for him that his gift—so perfect that she could still describe how badly she longed for it—was forgotten.

May we not come to a point in our lives where we can no longer take men-tal inventory of just how lucky we are, of just how good we have it. Instead, can we stop, realize all that we already have, and just give thanks? Can we live as thankful people?

PHILIPPIANS 4:8

"Whatever."

Said with a slight tone of disgust or disinterest, this word slips from the lips of a junior high teen. It's a dismissal, a way to let the hearer know he will no longer be heard. His input is being ignored. His existence is essentially extin-guished. After the utterance of this "whatever," never mind trying to make an impact—even a minor one—on the one who said it.

That is, unless, you are Paul writing to the church in Philippi. In his letter, he calls the readers to dwell on "whatever," but with a very different intent. Without ever using the word "thanks" Paul advises the readers to dwell upon all that makes them thankful.

"Whatever is true, whatever is honorable, whatever is just, whatever is pure, whatever is pleasing, whatever is commendable... think about these things."

Directing our attention toward the **essence** of thankfulness and not the **stuff** of it, Paul's take on thanks deviates strongly from that of our current time. Nothing listed here in verse eight is perishable. None of it has a shelf life, an expiration date, or a warranty. All of it simply exists, and is there for our appreciation if we choose to recognize it.

When I gather with the youth of my church group to talk about what they are thankful for, all sorts of **stuff** comes out—and it usually is **stuff**. In all fairness, first they mention their family and friends in general terms. But then, they offer extensive lists of their belongings, their things, their electronic toys, and their accumulated gadgets. They are thankful for what they can use, see, touch, break, replace, or throw away when they're done. In their defense, it's a learned skill, one the adult world around them has perfected and handed down. When parents ask their kids to write thank you notes for the material gifts they receive but not the kind acts they've witnessed, the adults promote this limited expression of thanks. The same lesson is taught when adults make money, not time for children, and then children receive presents, not presence from adults. And if tough financial times bring about few things to say thank you for, there must be nothing worthy of their thanks. Whatever.

And yet, somewhere in one's world there is something pure; there is at least a small patch of recognizable justice; there is honor. Paul calls us to recognize whatever is Christ-like in our surroundings and dwell on it. When we take into account this "whatever" that Paul calls us to, we will find cause for thanksgiving. If we are to make an account of thankworthiness in our days, these are the elements that need to be counted. Another way of thinking about it, these elements of "whatever," as Paul teaches, can make the person. We can be, not people whose stuff keeps breaking, but rather ones whose face glows in the recognition of all that is worthy of our appreciation.

Whatever is new on the market, whatever is best in the line, whatever is shiny, expensive, exclusive, let us not dwell on these, for they will not bring joy or satisfaction. Instead, see all that there is for which to be thankful: whatever is pure, true, honorable, and just. Find in these no expiration date and no disappointment.

3

THANKS FOR A FEW FISH AND A LITTLE BREAD

I attended Sunday School nearly every Sunday of my childhood, and so I figure I've heard or read the story of Jesus feeding the thousands about a thousand times. Sometime in my adult years, I began to wonder if Jesus actually transformed food from one boy's family into a feast for five thousand. Sometime later, I wondered if it mattered. Either way, Jesus gave thanks for what He had to share and God saw to it that everyone had enough. Could it be that the act of giving thanks for what we have will ensure that we have enough?

INSUFFICIENT CAUSE FOR THANKS

"Then Jesus took the loaves, and when He had given thanks, He distributed them to those who were seated; so also the fish, as much as they wanted."
John 6:1–14

Perhaps the greatest gratitude happens when the situation looks as if there is insufficient cause for thanks. When grandma shows up at your door with a box of cereal and a bag of marshmallows when you asked her to bring

Rice Krispies squares, it's hard to say thank you. When your "new" bike has a worn paint job and two flat tires, the words thank you are probably not the first things out of your mouth. When I asked for a drum set and my dad bought me a guitar instead, I wasn't feeling too thankful. Without knowing how these three situations might be resolved, there's little reason to feel thankful. Without faith in the people involved, disappointment is the mood of the moment.

There is a similar Gospel story where it appeared that there was insufficient cause for thanks, but Jesus said it anyways. When Jesus needed to feed thousands and was only offered a little bit of fish and bread, He thanked God. His was an act of pure faith: faith in the gift and its giver, faith in the disciples' potential, and faith in the crowds of people. In this event, Jesus demonstrates His faith that God would orchestrate matters into a miracle so powerful that it becomes one of the few recorded in all four gospels. The story can be found in John 6, Mark 6 and 8, Matthew 14 and 15, and Luke 9.

And so, it's in disappointing circumstances that near miracles sometimes develop. When Grandma takes time with just you in the kitchen to make a special treat together, then you feel grateful for the bag of marshmallows and the box of cereal. When your big brother shows you how to patch a tire, touch up a bad paint job, and then rides bikes with you all afternoon, then you can't stop singing his praises. Years later, when I could pack up my guitar, tote it with me everywhere and strum along with my friends, I was so thankful that I didn't get a drum set. Insufficient cause transforms into immeasurable glee. But being able to trust that there will be cause for thanks in the future is tough without faith.

With faith, though, many have said thanks in overwhelming circumstances. When we're in a hospital room with tubes and machines hooked up to someone we love, and we thank God, it's a thanksgiving of faith. When the job offer is for a minimum wage slot instead of the salaried position, and we thank God for the job that can't pay our daily expenses, those are words of faithful thanks. When we're out of gas and out of money to buy more gas, and we can thank God for a car, that's a thanks of faith. Perhaps the faith to respond with thanks in such situations comes from believing in gospel stories like this one.

TOO LITTLE, TOO LATE

"A large crowd kept following Him… When He looked up and saw a large crowd coming toward Him, Jesus said to Philip, 'Where are we going to buy bread for these people to eat?'" John 6:1–14

Too little, too late. How can one feel grateful for that? Maybe it's what I needed, but it's not nearly enough. Maybe it's what I wanted, but the timing is all wrong. How can I be expected to say thanks for that?

So we find the disciples here with too little and too late. The story is recorded in all four Gospels, varying slightly but with the same basic lesson. The disciples had retreated to a quiet place to be with Jesus. They did not fully receive what they wanted or needed. They were frustrated, and Jesus stayed cool.

In reading the story as recorded in John's Gospel, Jesus asks Philip where they can buy bread for the thousands of unexpected guests who followed them to this out-of-the-way place. Not in his exact words, Philip's reply may have gone something like this:

> "Come on, Jesus, it would take six months wages to feed all these people. We don't have that kind of money. And where exactly do you expect me to shop for all that? At the local convenient store? We're on a secluded hillside where we went in hopes of being left alone. If you want us to start up a new local bakery, then let's stop wandering around, settle in, and start baking."

Andrew is the next one to snap at Jesus. Again, I offer an imagined conversation, not his precise words: "Hey Jesus, here you go. A little kid over here has some old barley loaves, if you're really desperate, all of five loaves. Like that's going to help. Oh, I almost forgot, he's offering up his catch of the day too: two big fish. From the way it smells, he caught 'em last week. Let's see, that's one fish for every 2500 people. Thanks a bunch, kid."

But why are they so irritated? What's eating at these guys? I see at least three genuine reasons for the disciples to be at their wits ends because I too have felt angry in similar situations. First of all, this is a huge interruption for friends who just wanted time to be together. Some Gospel accounts have the twelve just returning from a missionary trip of their own. They were ready for some R&R, or at the very least some debriefing with their Rabbi. Instead, they were thrown into the role of hosts needing to feed a table of five times a thousand!

Secondly, they were offered insufficient resources for the task at hand. The disciples were wondering how to break five loaves into 5000 pieces. Jesus is dreaming big and the disciples are still stuck in the world of reality. They forgot that months before this, they had already seen Jesus perform this same miracle on another hillside with another crowd of thousands (see Matthew 14 &15 and Mark 6 & 8).

And then there is the insult of the food that was offered—barley bread. Apparently, this was the food of the very poor. Barley was the cheapest bread around and offering it to a crowd of thousands could set off a riot. Hungry people can be vicious. Alright, I may be exaggerating, but they may have been humiliated by this single offering of food from the crowd.

So what was Jesus' response? Was he insulted? Irritated by the interruption? Concerned about the insufficient meal? No. Jesus gave thanks to God, and then the meal began. In His words of thanks, the crowd, the disciples, and today's readers hear a different message.

In the interruption, Jesus found an opportunity. When seeking quiet and finding a crowd instead, Jesus' words of thanks show the value of every individual in that overwhelming mass of people. He transforms the interruption into a time for meeting physical, as well as spiritual needs.

With the seemingly insufficient food, Jesus saw generosity in a small boy. Jesus knew this little boy's example of selfless giving could stir an entire crowd into re-evaluating their own potential to give and share from their personal wealth or poverty. Jesus valued the boy's gift just as God valued every one of the people gathered on that hillside.

In the apparent insult, Jesus saw dignity and power. In giving thanks for the cheap bread of the poor, Jesus dignified their daily lives. In receiving the gift, thanking God for it, and proudly sharing it, He empowered a whole segment of society that was (and is) usually degraded and ignored. As some say, "God don't make junk," and Jesus knew the potential power in this bread.

Sometimes we see what we have as too little and too late. The same situation from Jesus' perspective could be plenty and timely. Jesus sees dignity, power, generosity, and opportunity when our lack of hopeful, faithful living sees cause for disappointment. Even when we, like the disciples, have seen where Jesus has previously helped us get through tough times, we think it'll be different this time—worse!

Maybe this story of thanks for some fish and bread can stick with us this time. Next time we feel like there's just not enough energy to get through the day, not enough patience to handle the situation, not enough funds to help support the needy, we could find encouragement from this story. Keep going with thanks for what we have. Maybe we'll find we have just what we need.

WHAT WE HAVE, WHO WE ARE AND WHERE WE ARE IN LIFE

The Gospel of John shares an amazing day of miracles when Jesus feeds thousands of people by miraculously multiplying a small amount of food gifted to Him by a small boy. There is certainly more than one miracle to be found in these verses. The obvious one is that Jesus fed thousands of people. Another is that there was food left over. Then there is the miracle of a poor boy giving over all that he had, thinking his very small gift could even make a difference. Did that gift inspire others to give more? Were the disciples miraculously transformed too, ready to serve the crowd? Could the miracles still be multiplying today as we reexamine this age-old story and hear its call to us? I hope so. With an eye toward thankfulness, where will this lesson lead us? This Bible story reminds me to be thankful for what I have, who I am, and where I am in life.

First, be thankful for **what we have**. When thinking about what we have, common knowledge tells us we don't have enough yet. And without enough, it's hard to share what we do have. If we follow the seemingly uncommon knowledge of thankful living, we may see ourselves as having enough—more than enough. Recognizing and appreciating our material gifts, personal giftedness, and the gift of family and friends, we can sense the overwhelming joy of having all we need. From this state, perhaps we'll be better suited to answer Jesus' request for food to feed the proverbial thousands, or at least share when called upon to do so. This story is a reminder that God is asking me to be thankful for what I have. And from my thankful stance, God knows that I will be better suited to share with others what they need.

In this story, Jesus miraculously multiplied the five loaves and inspired others to share from their own personal lunch boxes—is one any less of a miracle than the other? Sometimes getting us to see how much we already have is the miracle. And getting us to share it is another miracle! When we recognize what we already have, we find ourselves more willing to share our food and ourselves where needed.

Next, be thankful for **who we are**. There is a miracle to be found in a teacher who can open the eyes of a student to that student's own giftedness. In this story, Jesus wanted everyone present to be thankful for who they were by acknowledging their own giftedness. If I am grateful for who I am and see value in my talents, I want to share my talents and myself with God's people. An example can be found in the boy who came forward and offered his food to the disciples to share with the crowds that day. The boy was just that: a boy, a youngster, a child—a nothing in those times. But, Jesus saw more than that, and apparently, so did the child for he was the first one to come forward and offer himself and his catch of the day—just two fish—and some cheap bread. I think that kid was grateful for who he was and felt the joy of sharing himself with God's people. He could have been constrained by his youth, or his poverty, or the world's opinion of him as worthless. Instead, he gave from himself. What an inspiration! When we, like this boy, recognize how special we are, we are ready to give of ourselves.

Lastly, be thankful for **where we are in life**. The disciples were not happy with where they found themselves in that bible story. They had expected some down time alone with Jesus. They had wanted time to be fed, spiritually and emotionally. Instead, they found themselves called upon to feed others. In the Gospel stories, Jesus tells the disciples to seat the crowd, distribute the food, and then collect any remaining food. Here, Jesus shares with the twelve the call to leadership and love, encouraging them to be thankful for where they found themselves. Despite the interruption, the disciples had an opportunity before them to care, to lead, and to minister.

An early memory I have of being a mother involves this idea of being thankful for where I was in life. Although I had always dreamed of being a parent, I never realized all I would have to forfeit. The mother of an infant has so little time to herself, and so much of my regular activity was put on hold. I didn't run any more. I wasn't working outside the home. Meals were simpler. Visits with friends and family had multiple interruptions. Dave and I struggled to find quality time together. "Just wait," I told myself. "There will be time for that soon enough. Now it's time to be a mom. Be glad for these times."

Now I remember the first day of school this past fall when my children were out of the house by seven in the morning and wouldn't be home until five that evening. At the start of school, it's always a while before I receive a call to sub and so I was looking at a quiet few days—or weeks. I found myself with time to run, work, bake, visit, and share lunch with Dave. Even now, I miss the days of being with my little children, but it's time to be grateful for where I am at this point. I hope I can live up to my potential, see and use my gifts, and feed the hungry crowd if need be.

Finding meaning where we are today will allow us to be a part of another miracle yet to be seen. Appreciating what we have could open us up to the possibility of sharing more. Accepting who we are may prepare us to be the ones needed. Let's hope and pray that we are ready and willing to be where, what, and who God needs.

SHARING OUR OWN LOAVES AND FISH

"When they were satisfied, Jesus told His disciples, 'Gather up the fragments that are left over, so that nothing may be lost.' So they gathered them up, and from the fragments of five barley loaves, left by those who had eaten, they filled twelve baskets." John 6:1–14

Mother Teresa said, "If you can't feed a hundred people, then feed just one." The young boy who gave Jesus a few loaves and fish understood this noble instruction. Although the crowd numbered in the thousands, he offered what he had and Jesus saw it as sufficient. Jesus didn't say, "That's not enough! Boy, go get more where that came from." Instead, Jesus said thanks to God for the food, and then He broke it and shared it with the gathered crowd.

Mother Teresa's words, the little boy's actions, and Jesus' thanks speak to me. Nothing I have to offer is too small. If there is even a glimmer of good within me, I need to seize it, give thanks for it, and share it in whatever way this world needs it.

I am thankful for my smile. I will share it.

I am thankful for my job as a substitute. I look for students who need my smile and my help.

I am thankful for my home. I will welcome, with joy, those who come here.

I am thankful for the privilege of parenting. I will be the best parent I can be.

I am thankful for my wealth. I will seek ways to share it with others in need.

I am thankful for my writing skills. I will use these skills to encourage others to live their lives with thanks, too.

In sharing one's self, others may even be inspired to do the same. I think it was intentionally recorded that the boy's gift was more than enough to feed everyone there. There were enough leftovers to fill 12 baskets, one for each disciple. Wasting this gift of food, which Jesus had given thanks for, wouldn't have been an appropriate act. Perhaps the disciples' eyes were opened to their own offerings, their own gifts, their figurative loaves and fish they had to offer. Maybe the little boy's gift was meant to be an example to each of the disciples that they too were going to need to dig deep and see all that they could to share. Soon they would be without Jesus, and would be depending upon their own God-given talents to continue Jesus' ministry.

Whatever the personal few fishes and loaves may be for us as individual children of God, hopefully, we will recognize those and give thanks for them. Hopefully, we will have courage to offer those to Jesus when He makes the need known. And then, certainly, we will be a part of "feeding the thousands," or doing the work of God in these days. Even something that others may see as insufficient can be transformed into **food for thousands** when we give thanks for what we have to offer. And now, let's get out there and share it.

4

HEAVEN HERE ON EARTH

When I stand at the pearly gates of heaven, I imagine I will feel overwhelming thankfulness. But, why wait? There are times in our daily lives when we will glimpse the gates of heaven right here on earth. And there will be times when we'll have to defy the common ways of this world and earnestly seek, long and hard, for heaven's earthly encounters. In either case, be sure to acknowledge the necessity for gratitude.

THANKSGIVING IS AN ACT OF FAITH

"If we have faith in human kind, and respect for what is earthly, and an unfaltering belief in peace and love and understanding, this could be heaven here on earth." Lyrics by Tracy Chapman from the song, "Heaven's Here on Earth"

To live life looking for reasons to be thankful is to seek heaven here on earth. If we choose to be intentional about thankful living, we choose to be aware of heaven's brushes with earthly life. Rather than living for the hereafter, thankful living rejoices in the here and now. Thankful living is an expression of living faithfully.

A few specifics might be helpful here.

Jesus was offered only five loaves of cheap bread to feed thousands of people, and Jesus chose to thank God for that meager offering. He was in the business of being thankful and found cause for thanks in a situation that would cause most of us to curse heaven rather than send up our thanks. Because of His faith in God, Jesus graciously accepted a small gift and made it more than sufficient simply by saying, "thank you."

The apostle Paul found himself on a weather-beaten boat about to be torn to shreds by wicked, ragged rocks. In the midst of the storm, he called a timeout to break bread and thank God. Paul had become accustomed to seeking reasons for thanks when life was good and when his life was threatened. As he spoke his thanks, he influenced an entire crew and all its passengers to believe they had a future of hope. They were not disappointed, and they found dry land.

In all my wondering, I have never imagined heaven to resemble the inside of a large fish's belly. And yet, while residing in such a place, Jonah gave thanks to God for deliverance into the mess and smell of a whale. He was living and breathing his faith through a prayer that expressed his total trust in God.

Janet received the diagnosis of breast cancer and somehow she found cause for continued thankful living. She didn't want to stay home feeling sorry for herself; she said she wanted to get out and keep living and see God's presence. She lived her thanks.

Yes, Chuck lost his job. Yes, the times are tight and even a little frightening. And YES, God is good and so is life, and every day he volunteers for the park system. Heaven can be found even in the autumn fields of God's browning, drying, weathering flowers and plants. He says his thanks for his time in the fields with God's creation.

The biblical and personal examples above have several elements in common. These are people whose faith calls them to seek God and in so doing they find reason for thanksgiving. Even more amazing is this commonality: in each example, these folks give thanks before they know that everything will be all right. They say thank you before their needs are fully met.

Being thankful is an act of faith.

Jesus hasn't fed the crowd yet, but he still says thanks. Paul and his shipmates are not on dry land yet, but Paul gives thanks. Jonah is still in the sea, in the belly of a fish, and could be the fish's dinner at any moment, but Jonah says thanks. Janet thanks God for today not knowing if cancer will take her tomorrow. Chuck, without a job, thanks God before he is employed. For these people, saying thanks is a demonstration of their faith.

Faith is saying, "Thank you God for the sun," on a cloudy day. Faith is saying a dinner prayer of thanks when there is nothing left for another meal. Faith is being thankful for a safe journey that's not yet complete. Faith is thankfully seeing a slice of heaven in otherwise horrific surroundings. In the words of Tracy Chapman, "an unfaltering belief in peace and love and understanding, this could be heaven here on earth."

INDEED, IT WAS VERY GOOD!

"God saw everything that God had made, and indeed, it was very good."
Genesis 1:31

There are moments when I find myself in the midst of God's creation and I encounter heaven right there.

Last year, I received an unexpected invitation from Ohio Prairie Nursery, a locally owned business offering native seeds. It was a gorgeous late summer day and they wanted to pay me to walk through some of Northeast Ohio's most beautiful fields. They did ask me to work a little while out there, to carry pruning scissors and a gathering sack, to wear work gloves and harvest native seeds. They warned me of the dangers of clipping off a finger and getting bit by vicious field spiders. All a small price to pay for the privilege of preserving some of God's originals: native Ohio prairie grasses and flowers.

So I spent the day with one of my favorite people in the world, Emliss, and he taught me how to collect wingstem flower seeds. Ever since that day, I have admired the beauty of the "weeds" that grow along some roadsides, the splendid pigment splashed across some farm fields, and the brilliant color of fall flowers growing naturally around Ohio. I have a renewed appreciation for the beauty of God's world and the proximity of heaven. Thanks be to God for this awesome gift.

It gets me thinking, if I am grateful for something, am I more likely to care for it? If we recognize all God has created as good, are we more likely to look after God's creation? If in the world we see God's handiwork and are awed by it, will we then respect and look after it? The Genesis stories beautifully express God's love for all that God made—God saw that it was good. Likewise, if we see as God does, we'll acknowledge the world's value and we'll want to take better care of it. It all starts with being thankful for God's creation.

Do you remember as a child carefully stepping over the anthill so as to not smash any little ants? Or did you ever try to catch the fly buzzing through the house so you could release it outside rather than swat and kill it inside? The thought of eating a duck that my dad shot as it gracefully flew through the northern sky was more than my stomach could bear. Seeing an area clear cut of all trees for the first time made me want to stop using paper.

These reactions could be interpreted as respect for creation or as naive sentimentality. Closer examination of the Genesis story reveals that God instructs humans to subdue the earth and have dominion over its creatures. Can we care for and subdue it at the same time? Yes, I believe we can when we start with thanksgiving and respect for this good gift.

A good gift elicits thanks and use. A good gift is one we want to use, not just set in a corner to be admired. And yet, a good gift is one we want to preserve so that its goodness can be appreciated as long as possible. When we gave our daughter a special doll for her birthday, and she left it in the box for months, I was disappointed. On the other hand, we gave her an electronic bank, which she quickly used and broke. That disappointed me too. A point could be made here that I'm pretty hard to please, yes, but also that there is a balance between use and misuse of gifts. It's wrong to assume that Amy didn't fully appreciate our gifts because she didn't use them the way I wanted her to. And yet, isn't it appropriate to consider the gift giver's intentions when using a gift one has received?

What were God's intentions when God created the earth and then gave us dominion over it? The answer to this question must take into account that God considered all that was created as good. Furthermore, we might assume that God expects us to see all that is created as good, too.

Some of this may raise more questions than answers. And yet I am sure that seeking answers from an attitude of thanks will be more productive and closer to the way God wants us to respond.

GRANDMA'S SPECIAL TOUCH

Romans 1:20–25

Some of our childish understandings of faith permeate our adult concepts too. If God is in heaven, and if we can catch a glimpse of heaven here on earth, then, hey, we could see God right here and now! But if we can't see God here, how can we honestly be expected to believe in God's existence or offer our thanks? Paul reflected on this in his letter to the Romans. Paul wrote at the start of his letter that he was certain that all of humanity must be aware of God simply by existing in the world God created. And that simple awareness ought to lead them, and us, into honor and thanks to the Creator, our God.

As a child we only vacationed in one place, a very heavenly place for a child. Every summer for one week we traveled a whole day to a remote area of Canada on Georgian Bay to a small cottage owned by my grandparents and my aunt. Talk about not being able to miss the glory of our Creator—this is God's country! Fluffy white pillows of clouds and dreamy blue skies perpetually framed the dark blue water against the green pines and pink granite rock. But let me tell you about the real master of our Canadian stay: my grandmother.

The cottage was always spotlessly clean—even though it was in the remote wilderness. The "biffy," our outdoor toilet on a rock, was even perfectly decorated and never seemed to smell like one might expect an outhouse to. The cottage was decorated with home handoffs, items no longer needed or too worn for her Ohio home. Grandma managed to recreate their usefulness into a state suitable for the front cover of *Better Homes and Gardens*. Speaking of gardens, each little crack and crevasse of the rock our summer villa was situated on was oozing with sweet summer annuals, dotting the already picturesque scene with bursts of color and warmth. The meals were more than plentiful; they were delicious, fulfilling, and homemade. Being at the cottage in Canada was like being engulfed by grandma Haynam; her touches were everywhere.

After more than 25 years away, my family stayed in the cottage the past two summers. My cousin's family has renovated and restored the cottage, which sat empty for years. Now, there is a washhouse with a flush toilet and even a shower—no more bathing in the lake! The inside was scrubbed and cleaned and updated with some new bedding. And yet the entire week I kept expecting to see my grandma, even though she died 22 years ago. The proof of her loving presence was still evident in almost everything I touched or saw there. There were pictures on the walls, dishes in the cupboards, books on the shelves, even a jacket and hat on the coat hooks.

Is this the essence of Paul's point in these verses of Romans? We live in the midst of God's cottage, where all we see, taste, hear, smell, and feel are evidence of God's creating power and presence. Others make efforts to renovate or alter God's creation, but God's staying power is resilient. Ignoring this and choosing to believe the beauty's source is something other than Godly is erroneous. Paul is pretty harsh in his treatment of those who choose to overlook the honor due to the Creator. Paul wants us to realize there is potential pain in making light of one's responsibility to thank God. However, let us learn a life lesson from his words: We need to give thanks where thanks is due, and we need to be aware daily of God's creative power.

Praising the creature instead of the Creator (verse 25) is a limited view that can lead to the formation of a false reality, in which all we enjoy we think is of our own making. We think that if we've made it all, we can recreate it all too. But we cannot recreate the earth in its precious balance. God orchestrated this earth's function and we don't have all the pieces in place to remake it. The love in a human heart can be seared and torn to shreds even if the physical heart can be replaced or repaired by the hands of a surgeon. The time we've used or wasted is gone and cannot be remade even though God can forgive and cover the errors of the past unlike anything we can do for one another. The creature, as smart as we are, cannot match the creative staying power of our Creator!

And so what is there to do other thank say, 'thank you."

The words of yet another song, by Jaroslav J. Vajda, speak of the presence of heaven here on earth and of our feeble attempts to express our thanks, "God of the sparrow, God of the whale, God of the swirling stars... How does the creature say Awe? How does the creature say Praise? God of the rainbow, God of the cross, God of the empty grave... How does the creature say Grace? How does the creature say Thanks?"

5
TEAMWORK!

Our family is fully plugged into the potential power of teamwork. Because of the sports our kids play, we've experienced the success of a team that is grateful for each team member. And we've experienced the devastation of gratitude-deficient teams, too. Likewise, there is power in appreciating the synergy found in loving others, God, and self, as a team.

A GREAT TEAMMATE

God is my jogging partner, a teammate. As I run laps around the indoor track, God is the one who I talk to all the while and the one who challenges me to keep up the good fight. With God's help, I not only keep up my pace on the track, I keep up my good work in my daily challenges. This relationship seems to be working well for us. I don't count on God to do all the work for us; we're in it together. I try to be quick to acknowledge God's participation and God's support while also being aware of my ability to contribute.

What if we mistakenly view God as a referee rather than as a teammate? As referee, God is the one on the court making bad calls against our team and missing push offs, moving picks, and flying elbows thrown in our faces by the other team. We look for a coach to negotiate with the ref from the sidelines. We await the fans' jeering complaints against the ref, hoping they'll effect his calls. And at the game's end, we scapegoat the ref for our loss, rather than recognizing our own poor effort. Never is there a word of thanks for the game's ref. Folks in the gym don't catch the ref making all the fair calls. Rarely is his skill acknowledged.

Having a thankful attitude toward a game referee is unlikely, and so seeing God as a ref is unwise. God's not calling out infractions against us as if we were players on the court of life. God is not watching from the sidelines, hoping to catch us doing wrong. Rather, our God is radically in our favor, actively playing the game of life with us and showering us with blessings. We could be the ones making the calls. So, call them blessings, good plays, gifts, a part of life, but, make the call! Give them name and notice. See cause for thanks! See all the game's opportunities and see God as a player right there with us.

Recognize God as a team player, someone in the game striving for a win along with us. God gives us a good pass, and we have a chance at the lay up. God places the pick that helps us around that defensive wall, and we're at the hoop. God brings the ball down the court, analyzes the set up, and calls the play, if we're listening. And God puts the three-point play in place for the win. We just need to see God's participation on the team. Recognize God's skill; see all the possibility God has placed before us, every time that orange ball makes its way into our hands.

The good in life is as varied as the number of plays available to a good team. Some consider new cars and big houses as good blessings. Others see the joy of a simple life and undisturbed nature as gifts. There is pleasure in solitude and independence. There is revelry in family and a large circle of friends. The crucial point is the recognition of the good plays and of God as a part of it all! See the thankworthiness of where we stand and follow that up by thanking God for being in the game with us. We can make a great team.

A WORD OF THANKS FOR YOU, AND YOU AND YOU ...

My daughter has become quite a team player. She is very protective of all the girls on her teams, as well as the coaches. If I have a negative comment about a player's attitude, she'll come to her defense. No point in mentioning an error that someone made in the last game; Amy will quickly set me straight. She is thankful for every player and finds the good in each one.

What would happen if every time we encounter anyone, we would, like Amy, find the good in them and silently say a prayer of thanks to God for that person? Would it change the way we interact with people and make us into team players too? And what if we mentioned to God specifically what it is about that person we are thankful for? Our thanks wouldn't be rote words of habit, but genuine thoughts of gratitude for each person.

In the introductions to his letters, Paul generally starts with words of thanks for the people he writes to. I love his expressions of gratitude. Read these:

"… because your faith is proclaimed throughout the world." (Romans)

"… because of the way the grace of God has been given to you." (I Corinthians)

"… for in every way you have been enriched in Christ, in speech and knowledge of every kind." (I Corinthians)

"… because of your sharing in the gospel." (Philippians)

"… for we have heard of your faith… and the love that you have." (Colossians)

"… because of the hope laid up for you in heaven." (Colossians)

"… your work of faith and labor of love and steadfast hope in our Lord Jesus Christ." (I Thessalonians)

"… because your faith is growing abundantly." (II Thessalonians)

"… the love of everyone of you for one another is increasing." (II Thessalonians)

"… because I hear of your love for all the saints and your faith toward the Lord Jesus." (Philemon)

All of these people are ones I want on my team. In Paul's expressions of thanks for them, we see his hope for them as children of God. As the letters continue, he has lessons to teach and admonishes some communities for their errant ways. But, he started with the good, the beautiful, and the hopeful. It made his tough message a little easier to swallow. Perhaps it made

Paul choose to express himself more kindly because he was starting with a kind heart himself. His inspiration for writing was love and faith, not anger or disappointment.

When I sit to write a note of thanks to someone, generally it's for something they have done for me specifically. It's for a gift they've given, a kind act they performed, generosity they offered to me. As I select a thank you card, I am picturing the recipient and choosing a card design I think they will appreciate. I try to write in a style appropriate for that person, relating my words to their kindness.

My daily interaction with people is not always so carefully thought out. But what if it was? What if I approached each interaction as an expression of gratitude for having the opportunity to share with that person? Whether it was a ride to ball practice with my daughter or a purchase from the clerk at the local convenience store, each opportunity for exchange could be an expression of appreciation for that person.

When we are with those we know well, there are attributes that readily come to mind, bringing thanks to our hearts for them. Of course, there are causes for aggravation too, but we decide which attributes to dwell on. And with those we do not know well or don't know at all, we can begin a practice of finding cause for thanks for them. I am glad when the clerk is there working and the store is open when I need to shop. I am glad for those who actually smile, say hello, and look me in the eye. I am glad for the people who take their work seriously, even when that seriousness translates into a stern demeanor. I can choose to be grateful for the stranger who drives carefully even when it delays me. I can patiently be thankful for the elder who moves slowly when I am in a hurry or the child who talks with enthusiasm when being quiet is more appropriate. Giving thanks for others puts me in a better frame of mind when I interact with them.

Actually saying thanks out loud to each person I see today may be a bit unrealistic. But, I can thank God, quietly in my heart, for folks who share my day. I might even go further and, like Amy, come to the defense of the one I hear criticism about, reminding others, and myself, of the good I see in that individual. And who knows, I might even be able to see cause for thanks and say thanks for a stranger I see today. Thank you for your smile. Thank you for holding the door. Thank you... and you... and you...

ACCOMPLISHMENTS OF A COMMUNITY

"Now at the dedication of the wall of Jerusalem they sought out the Levites… to celebrate the dedication with rejoicing, with thanksgiving and with singing, with cymbals, harps, and lyres." Nehemiah 12:8, 27–31, 43

A few summers ago, our little Northeast Ohio town dedicated a new playground. The dedication took place on July 4, traditionally the biggest day of celebration in the little village of Hiram. There is a parade with more kids on bikes than spectators, children's games on the lawn, an annual tug-o-war contest, old vs. young softball game, bike rodeo, an ice cream social, and two band concerts—one with dancing under the stars. Some years we even have fireworks. On this one special year we added the dedication of a beautiful new play space for all the children in the area.

The celebration included words from our mayor—of course—recognition of the primary philanthropist, and my favorite part, words from the coordinator of all the efforts, Ken. One of the world's most positive people, Ken gave thanks to all present with his most sincere gratitude for the many folks who contributed their time and money to our village playground. Those of us who personally know Ken realized that none of us would have been able to pull off such a terrific civic endeavor without his jovial and wise leadership and vision. We also knew that he was planting the last of the park's flowers the morning before!

As usual, Ken didn't want the recognition, but he created a way that others could give their thanks. Contributors donated paving bricks that were laid into a walkway leading from the park's car lot to the playground. During the dedication Ken didn't read each individual brick, but encouraged us to do so and to thank those named in the bricks. For well over an hour, I watched as folks wondered the pathway, heads down and pointing at bricks. They were recognizing names of others who, like Ken, love children and bought a brick to ensure a place dedicated to the fine art of child's play.

His efforts that day encouraged our little town, as our children played, giggled, and squealed with joy throughout the dedication ceremony. We saw a dream made into a reality in this little place of play in a world of too much worry. That day we all patted ourselves on the back and hugged Ken for giving us a reason to become child-like.

Like Ken, Nehemiah wanted to encourage the residents of his town. As governor, he helped them build a new wall around the city. And also like Ken, Nehemiah wanted to restore the city of Jerusalem to a more lovely state. He wanted more than a wall; Nehemiah strove for a renewed respect for the Sabbath, for the poor, and for Jewish law. When the wall was complete, the party was planned and the official men of thanks were recruited to lead the celebration.

Here is where the two stories diverge somewhat. Hiram celebrated the efforts of its own wonderful citizens. Jerusalem celebrated God—their rejoicing was for God (verse 43). Some say it took only 52 days to build that wall. Some say it was at least 60 feet tall. But on that day of celebrating, all said their thanks to God.

The Hebrew faithful took their thanksgiving seriously. In fact, they had a whole tribe dedicated to praising God with songs of thanksgiving, instruments of rejoicing, and companies of singers. These were the Levites and for this special day they were rounded up from all the surrounding towns and villages and brought into Jerusalem to lead the praise processions around the new wall. Nehemiah describes the way the Levites divided into two great companies, one going left and one going right to engage the whole city in the day's purpose. On that day "the joy of Jerusalem was heard far away," like the happily squealing children of Hiram.

I wonder who organized the rebuilding efforts? Who oversaw this great engineering feat? Who dragged the stones and lifted them into place? Who fed the workers? Who tended to their wounds? Who went out into the neighboring villages to find the Levites? Who was their Ken? Not one of them had their names carved into a paving brick.

For that day, all the praise went to God. I wonder if any of them felt overlooked? Did they want a share of the praise? Were they longing for a moment that Nehemiah would thank them personally? Or were they satisfied to be a part of something bigger than anyone of them, something that recognized the glory of God?

I can recall a few times when accounting for my personal efforts meant nothing to me because I was so overwhelmed with gratitude to God. It's an attitude I ought to be striving to duplicate more often. Too often I recognize the work I have done to keep this household going, overlooking the dedication of my family members. I have been known to complain to my kids for sitting around doing nothing only to be reminded of all that they already did do that day. Muttering to myself about needing to arrive early to work only to find other co-workers diligently plugging along—with a smile on their faces. Oh yeah, others are making this all work too, aren't they?

Perhaps in acknowledging that a task is bigger than a single person, a community can contribute to an accomplishment that benefits many. Perhaps my friends Ken and Nehemiah have the right idea. **Involve** many. **Expect** no personal glory. **Be ready** to thank and celebrate the accomplishment of the community! And be sure to bring your cymbals!

GRACE. PERIOD.

"Yes, everything is for your sake, so that grace, as it extends to more and more people, may increase thanksgiving, to the glory of God." II Corinthians 4:15

A few years ago, Dave and I boarded a ship in Seattle for a four-day cruise to Victoria, British Columbia where we visited a different port city each day. Let me tell you, getting on and off the boat each day was a BIG deal. Before one day's excursion, we stood waiting nearly two hours for all the proper arrangements to be made for our group to leave the boat. And getting on the boat? We found you better not be late, you better have all your documentation, and you better use the sanitizer squirted into your hands by the ship's crew. Getting on and off a cruise ship is no vacation! I don't fully understand what all the fuss was about, but I followed the rules with very little thanks for the inconvenience.

Grace is another one of those concepts I don't fully understand. In this verse from his second letter to the Corinthians, Paul throws this word around simply assuming its meaning is already deeply embedded in the reader's faith vocabulary. And what does grace have to do with thanks? Paul explains: as grace is recognized by more of us, more of us will be thankful. If we don't understand what grace is, we won't appreciate it and we'll miss the thanksgiving boat. Now, we know you don't want to miss the boat. So let's try to figure out this grace thing and get on board!

Speaking **not** as a theologian, but as a seeker just trying to pull her faith together, here is what I think about grace. Grace is like winning a contest because the deciding panel members are all in love with me. Grace is like having the game's ref on my side! But then again, it's not quite like these two examples because I don't think grace has any losers. Let me try again.

Grace is like mom and dad picking me up as a raging, screaming child in the midst of a tantrum and smothering me with hugs and kisses. It's when grandma loves me even after I've broken the heirloom candy jar. Grace is making the team even though my skill today doesn't warrant it.

Grace is like a judge telling the prosecuting attorney to sit down and shut up. The judge doesn't even want to hear the charges against me; I've already been forgiven.

Grace is seeing a beautiful sunrise after a night of wild carousing. It's hearing a glorious songbird when I'm in the midst of yelling at my children. Grace is finding the love of my life and knowing that he loves me even though I haven't been a such a good, loving human being. Grace is being loved, not earning love.

There are dictionaries that help those of us who are twenty-first century readers agonizing over Paul's first century theological terms. One such book is *The Dictionary of Bible and Religion.* In that resource, grace is defined in part as "God's free and loving regard for humankind expressed in all God has done and continues to do for all men and women as **sinners** and as **God's people**" (p. 407). The explanation continues to define grace in the New Testament as, "God's kindly attitude to men and women, bestowing on them pardon and receiving them into God's family as **unworthy** but **beloved** children" (p. 408). The painful part of these definitions is being called "sinner" and "unworthy." The feel-good part is being recognized as "beloved" and as "God's people." Understanding the deep significance of grace means we recognize both the painful and good as parts of who we are. We appreciate the fact that grace transforms us from unworthy sinners into beloved children! When we comprehend this as gift, our whole being will radiate with thanks for our God. It's a realization that God is surely on our team.

Some collection agencies allow for a grace period. It's a short time during which a debtor may repay an overdue amount. When the grace period expires, the debtor is out of luck and will owe the debt **plus** additional interest, compounding daily! God's grace is nothing like a grace period. God's grace is more like: Grace. **Period.** If we can wrap our heads around that concept, thanksgiving will increase. And to God will be the glory. And for us, we'll never miss the thanksgiving boat.

REMEMBER TO BE THANKFUL FOR YOURSELF

It's been 30 years now since I met Tracy. She was new to our community, new to the large high school, and new to our church youth group. She was a spunky, redheaded 15 year old with a strong dose of self-confidence—but not cocky. She wasn't going to go unnoticed in the world, that's for sure.

Tracy wanted to join the church. She didn't really have any church experience and our pastors wanted her to know what she was committing to. But, she was also older than all the 13-year-olds in the confirmation class where most youth learned about church membership. I was a relatively young youth worker, just seven years older than Tracy, but with a strong faith and a willingness to share it with her. I was already helping with the confirmation class, familiar with the teaching material. It was a good match. Tracy and I were going to try an experiment. We would try a tutoring set up, meeting once a week to discuss faith issues and church membership at a level more suited to a high school student.

We met in Tracy's home, on the porch. She'd offer me iced tea and I'd offer her my perspective on faith. She'd share a smile and a laugh and I'd share my understanding of the Bible. She'd tell me what happened at school that day and I'd tell her what happens in a church of devoted members. We met throughout the spring, maybe two months.

Sometimes the lessons would go off-track and it was wonderful. Tracy's questions were heartfelt and genuine. And when I was the one asking the questions, her answers were sincere, expressing her faith and her confusion. The time together went quickly. The last official gathering was met with disappointment on my part. I learned so much from my student and wasn't convinced that I had offered as much to her. The relationship seemed off-balance. Had we switched roles: Tracy the teacher, I the student? Internally, I felt I failed her.

In all her maturity, Tracy diminished my disappointment with a simple card and a bookmark. The card expressed her thanks for our times together and how it opened her to a growing faith. The bookmark she made herself, cross-stitching a sunlit cross and the following words: "Lord teach us joy in the simple things." She signed the back.

For a time, I forgot to be thankful for myself because seeing her confidence as a high school student reminded me of what I wasn't. But then her words of thanks reminded me of just who I was, a child of God, giving what I could, when I could, to whom I could. And that is enough. In fact, that is beautiful. In giving Tracy my best and recognizing her best, I was the face of God for her. What more can we ever ask for in this life?

I'd love to tell you how Tracy and I maintained contact all these years and continued to share our faith as I watched her grow into a young woman. We didn't. Her father's job moved them to another town, another school, and hopefully another church where she continued to grow in faith and share her love. I no longer have the heartfelt card she gave me, but the bookmark is still a treasured gift.

That experience was one of the several that year that propelled me into ministry. I began to recognize my potential. Time with Tracy helped me say thanks for me. Being thankful for oneself is an indispensable part of thankful living.

Most of us have had the experience of being with people who aren't feeling so good about themselves. I notice it when I hear someone pointing out his accumulated electronic assets such as a new phone, an updated sound system, and ipod, as if these acquisitions will finally earn him the respect he longs for. Someone else may verbally berate herself, hoping someone within earshot will throw a lifeline compliment to pull her up from her sea of self-hate. And then there are those who reject every compliment we offer, as if not worthy of any appreciation. All of these are folks who lack the self-love needed to simply say, "Thanks for me!" How do we recognize our own self-worth?

Not one of us will be the best at everything. Very few of us will be the best at any one thing. And so searching for self-worth by comparing ourselves to others is a surefire way to worthlessness. Some people will achieve their personal best in a certain area, although actually knowing when we are the best we can be is difficult to measure—to say the least. This may not be the most effective way of finding self-worth either. Working as hard as we can to impress others can't guarantee their satisfaction. Some people will never be satisfied and will always want more from us. Pleasing others can be an elusive endeavor.

To find an internal center of self-love requires recognition of one's personal value, as well as the value of all other humans. I will thank God for you and recognize your talents and gifts. I will thank God for me and my talents and gifts. No, make that even more basic. I will thank God for you. Period. And I will thank God for me. Period. Enough said.

6

TO GRIPE OR GIVE THANKS

Without a doubt there will be times that leave us complaining. However, is it possible that the effort expelled for the sole purpose of griping is effort unavailable for gratitude? It might be that when times are tough, the tough find cause for thanksgiving!

I DON'T DESERVE THIS!

"Let them thank the Lord for God's steadfast love, for God's wonderful works to humankind." Psalms 107

My friend Pete is convinced that every time he returns to church, things go bad. He explains that throughout his life he has been in and out of active church participation. Over the years he's found the drive to return to church life and to attend worship weekly. He begins to pray again. He serves the church and the community as an expression of growing faith. He even joins church committees! And then something really bad happens. He brother is stricken with cancer. He leaves church, angry with God. Then later, he returns. His young niece is raped. He leaves. He returns. He loses his job and his dog dies. He leaves and reluctantly returns, again and again. As he sees the turn of events, somehow God is testing him each time he tries to come back into the fold. He has made a mental and spiritual connection between his church attendance and his life's catastrophes.

This painting of Pete's life, as he tells it, is an incomplete picture. There are daily stokes of color and vibrancy that he is blinded to. He fails to recognize the good that came his way too, like the months of remission that his brother had, the child psychologist who helped his niece, the new job he has, supportive neighbors, a wedding anniversary, his daughter's graduation, paid off loans, functioning cars, delicious dinners, and a new friend. Deep Christian fellowship, sustaining worship, loving friends, daily breath, and nightly rest are joys of every day living that he has forgotten to include in his story.

In no way do I mean to minimize the suffering that Pete and his family have suffered, pain that I have never had to endure in all my years. I only wonder if maybe credit needs to be given where credit is due. And God deserves some credit for the blessings we enjoy too. Personally, I am not one to assume that God is testing me when I'm going through bad times. But if that is one's understanding of God's character, than maybe we're being tested when we enjoy good times, too. God wants to know if we'll say thanks as readily as we'll say no thanks. Will we give thanks to God as readily as we will gripe to God?

Psalms 107 recounts tragedy faced by various people when life gets real hard. The people cry to God, and God responds with aid. I can hear the Psalmist pleading for people's recognition of the good times they are now experiencing once they have been rescued from their affliction. It's as if the Psalmist is saying, "Hey, remember to say thank you! Remember how awful you felt before. Remember you believed there was no hope. Remember you thought you were done for and you complained, and wined, and cried about it. Well, now that you are living the good life—live it thankfully!" Actually, the verse that is repeated four times (verses 8, 15, 21, and 31) is, "Let them thank the Lord for God's steadfast love, for God's wonderful works to humankind!"

Like Pete, all of us can get caught in a blame game, asking God why such bad stuff has to happen. Do we ever question why all the good stuff happens? I am reminded of the inspiring words of my friend Jean Henthorn, a woman in her 80s. When asked how she is doing, Jean replies something like this, "I haven't done anything to deserve all this. What I mean is, I don't deserve this endless stream of blessings God has sent my way." Jean has seen more than her fair share of hardship, but all she's recounting are the continued reasons to sing God's praise and say thank you. Perhaps her life story is comparable to Pete's. One has chosen to gripe. The other has chosen to give thanks. I guess we all have a choice in how we will respond to life.

SNOOPY IS BARKING

The *Peanuts* characters, created by Charles Schultz, bring me massive amounts of joy. Their little stories, round heads, personalities and personal flaws, and reoccurring mistakes and misunderstandings ring true to reality for me. Most importantly, *Peanuts* makes me smile.

Snoopy is my favorite. For reasons I can't begin to understand or explain, I can fully relate to this dog. Is that a bad thing? I didn't have a real dog as a child, but somehow imagined that Snoopy was mine. When reading the daily comic and finding Snoopy as the feature character, I felt as though a member of my family had made the paper. However, now that I actually do have a dog, I find few similarities between my dog, Basil, and my childhood fantasy dog, Snoopy. All that changed recently.

I have a daily *Peanuts* calendar that sits on my desk, giving me cause to laugh every day. A recent comic featured my Snoopy, usually a light-hearted, quiet dog, out of sorts and barking for no apparent reason. Not only was Snoopy barking, Charlie Brown, the dog's real owner, explained that he knew that type of bark. It was Snoopy's "barking just for the sake of it" bark! My dog does that! My Basil barks for no apparent reason, just like Snoopy did in that comic. Now, is that a bad thing?

If these two dogs bark for no apparent reason, maybe Basil will start mimicking Snoopy in other, more endearing ways. Maybe she'll start dancing with reckless abandon. Maybe Basil will begin to nuzzle us for a warm hug. Perhaps she'll even strike up a friendship with cute little yellow birds. I am now hopeful that my Basil could become like Snoopy in these lovable ways.

Do you know folks who "bark" for the sake of barking? Do you find them to be less lovable? These might be the ones who gripe daily. They complain about the leaves falling. They groan about the rising price of milk. They bemoan the heat and then the cold. They remember the good 'ole days when the church pews were full. They whine about the nasty team coach or the miserable co-worker. Then they start in on the people they're supposed to love. They don't like her cooking or his housekeeping skills. They're angry their kids haven't called all week. After a while, it's just like the irritating noise of an incessantly barking dog and we listen to it with just as much intensity. In other words, we try to tune it all out.

I know a lovely elderly lady whose mere presence is like soothing poetry. Her voice, her calm presence, her gentle smile, and her sincere eyes have no hit of a bark in them. Elizabeth finds cause for living with purpose and thankfulness everyday. Some would think she has reason to grouch: her health is failing, her ability to create art is fading, her beloved husband has died, and she suffered a house fire. Yet, Elizabeth continues to take in the blessings of life and radiate love for life. When I grow up, I want to be just like Elizabeth.

This desire to be like my friend requires practice and daily preparation. For instance, when I hear myself barking, I better make sure I have ample cause. There are times when a good bark can grab others' attention and lead to desired results. However, complaining without a plan for conversion is just like an annoying, ceaseless bark. Already in my 50s, if I hope to grow into the kindly manner I witness in my mature friend, Elizabeth, I want to be sure my tone is veering toward gentle-speak and not sharp-tongue. She has avoided the pitfalls of a life of growling, snarling, yipping, and howling and instead offers a life of song, poetry, and pleasantries.

I find thankful living is key to minimal, unnecessary barking. If I choose to look at the world with an eye for the good, the hopeful, and the joyful, I will find myself overcome with reasons for thanks. And when in a thankful state, I find a song in my heart and the energy for continuing the good and creating more joy for others.

In that recent comic, Snoopy was barking for the sake of barking. In another strip, he's a beloved companion and friend for Charlie Brown. Each of us, like my Basil, will have days of too much barking. Then again, each of us, like Snoopy, can start a new day with new reasons to smile and bring joy to others. It's a hopeful way to interpret our days and it's the way any one of us can choose to live. Now, is that a bad thing?

KNIT TOGETHER

"You knit me together in my mother's womb. I give thanks to You, for I am fearfully and wonderfully made." Psalms 139:13–14 (NASB)

There are times when it's easier for me to see God's creative wisdom when viewing a simple flower rather than looking in the mirror or examining my résumé, my checkbook, or any other measure of my value. It's painful to admit that I will deny God's creative indulgence in my conception. But that is exactly what I am doing—consciously or subconsciously—when I self-deprecate or minimize my worth and gripe about who I am.

Coming to terms with our need to thank God for all of life includes giving thanks for who we are, how we look, and what we are capable of. The Psalmist states God's creative part in our birth in this Psalm: we have been wonderfully, fearfully made, knitted together, woven and formed, not hidden from God.

As a Camp Fire girl, our troop spent several weeks trying to learn how to knit. I was lost within an hour when we had to wind the yarn into a uniform ball. My ball of red yarn was askew, with loops loosely falling from the mass. The following week, the knitting needles wouldn't hold the yarn in place as I repeatedly dropped one stitch after another. I never finished my knitting project. It's a good thing that God never gave up on the knitting project called Pamela.

The Psalmist's choice of the word "knit" is painfully real to me and I know it requires care, concentration, intention, and love. I envision God as a grandmotherly character, sitting comfortably in an old, wooden rocking chair, setting each stitch into place, envisioning the desired shape and size, never feeling hurried or bored, and already loving the finished project. As God knitted my son and my daughter, there were folks knitting handmade baby blankets to celebrate their births. For me, each blanket gifted to our children continues to be a reminder of God's involvement in the careful knitting of every child. Hopefully, I have lived my days expressing my belief in every child's worth as a creation of God and helping those kids see their worth. In order to be true to that message, I should have also demonstrated an appropriate measure of care, love, and respect for myself.

Loving oneself is seeing one's potential. It's being just a little biased, knowing one is capable of something a little more challenging. It's a fine line to walk.

Viewing myself as better than others isn't helpful either because my attitude will stain those relationships. Instead, seeing that I am a good, worthy person, created in God's image gives me the enthusiasm to recognize my worth and push myself to do better, to try harder, and stretch further toward my potential.

While in middle school, our daughter Amy earned fourth place in a writing contest. Competing against 75 other high-ranking students from nine area schools, our family praised her accomplishments. For quite some time, I suspected that Amy had special talents in the area of creative writing, but this was a wonderful confirmation of my belief and her talents. We presented her with a rose, placed her trophy prominently in the living room, bought her an ice cream treat, and took her out for dinner, too! We called her grandparents as soon as we got home and relived the day's events with them. Later that night, while praising her for the umpteenth time, Amy replied, "I think I am going to have a tough time living this down." She was recognizing her potential.

In this moment, Amy saw a glimpse of who she was becoming. It was one of those times when she looked within and saw herself as a wonderfully made child of God, carefully woven into not just a good athlete, not just a pretty young teen, not just a girl with fun friends. Amy is a young woman with talents that God will continue to cultivate and encourage. Those kinds of moments can be the ones that buoy us up when the world's accolades are not being showered on us. These are times when our internal ledger builds and the dividends accumulate, preparing us for a possible, future recession. These are the times we see through the glass clearly, not dimly (I Corinthians 13:12), distinctively beholding what we can become.

The recent rash of suicides due to bullying make me feel sick and more than just sad. Perhaps these young people believed more in the hatred they heard than in the potential they held. We, as a society, were not able or did not try hard enough to build up these young people. They were not yet convinced of their worth, their value, or their personal power. And what of the ones who participated in the bullying? Where was their sense of self-worth? A healthy dose of self-love creates loving characters capable of seeing the value in others. In recognizing that one is wonderfully made by a caring Creator, she will live knowing that all others have likewise been lovingly and wonderfully made, and therefore worthy of her respect.

Recognizing the glory in the world around us is vital in living fully each day. Giving thanks for our internal glory makes us fit for living our days as God's ambassadors. As such, we see and know our individual beauty and recognize the beauty in all of God's creation and children.

THANKS FROM THE BELLY OF A FISH

Jonah 1 and 2

Here is a prayer of thanks in the Scripture that starts from the third day in the belly of the fish. And what, exactly, is there to be thankful for when a person finds himself in the belly of a fish? On the third day?

And why would he give thanks to the being that put him there in the first place? As Jonah sees it, it was God who threw him into this watery mess—although the sailors are the ones who picked him up and pitched him over in an effort to stop the raging sea. Jonah doesn't place blame on the sailors, but he clearly states that God cast him into the heart of the sea. How can he see the need to thank God from the internal mire of a fish's belly when God is responsible for his present state?

Jonah is apparently ready to start again with God, and a good place to start is with thanks. Where else could Jonah start? At this point he could start with blame— understandably. Or how about anger? Jonah could start with self-pity, defiance, rage, or even confusion. Making a new start with thankfulness seems ridiculously out of place, but it's a great example for us all. True, it may have taken Jonah three days in the belly of the fish to get to this point. But some of us haven't reached that point in a lifetime.

If every time I became angry with someone or a situation, I had to sit for three days by myself, perhaps then I would find reasons for gratitude. In other words, given the opportunity to really focus on the circumstances that surround my situation I bet I would generally see that others are not to blame for where I am but that I am. And usually I would come to see that things are pretty good, maybe even downright wonderful. Forced into a time of reflection by myself I hope that I too, like Jonah, might find that life is really good. I might start counting my blessings instead of tallying the offences against me, which I tend to do when rushing through life, busy with things that are oh-so-important.

There are external forces that tend to add to one's negativity, creating more reasons to grumble about how awful things are. The world will readily add to our "woe is me" wagonload of complaints, worries, and tallies of injustices. But if we could, like Jonah, sit in the belly of the proverbial whale for a few days, without all those external voices adding to our list of grievances, we might actually be able to start counting our blessings. Since not many of us can regularly get away from the world for three days, we might want to look for other options.

When found with a thankless heart, we need to give ourselves a few moments to reflect on the possibility of good. Stop and smell the roses—this old cliché holds a long history of truth. Snatch a few seconds of "fish belly time" where the complaints of the world are ignored and the beauty of life is relished. "Fish belly time" might be those extra minutes in bed, after hitting the snooze button, when we think of three things to be thankful for (a friend tells me each morning he's just glad that he's not six feet under). It might be the time during a car commute when we turn off the radio and find something pretty to lift our spirits: a shiny car, commuters with smiles on their faces, kids on bikes, a sea of green trees, the absence of emergency sirens. Fish belly opportunities may present themselves when waiting in lines, or waiting for appointments, or waiting to fall asleep. Just be sure to turn off the receptors that seek negativity.

Let's be honest here, even though it's hard to hear. Sometimes those "external voices" are too close to home. Sometimes they are not externally sourced at all. Sometimes we are our own worst enemy and we give ourselves more and more cause for unhappiness. Maybe sitting alone for three days would not bring us to Jonah's place of gratitude. Then what? How do we get away from our griping selves?

We cannot get away from ourselves. Instead, we have to get inside ourselves and do some reorganizing. Just as we might force ourselves into a new exercise regiment, if the negativity is coming from within, we'll have to follow a thankful heart exercise. We may need to force feed ourselves thankful thoughts just like we would force feed ourselves fruits and vegetables when starting a new diet. When not able to escape the world for three days we might have to make ourselves go through the motions of thankfulness until the motions become authentic actions.

The lessons from the Jonah tale remind us that (1) we are often at fault for the situations in which we find ourselves, (2) upon closer examination there is good cause to give God thanks, and (3) that three days of fish belly time might be what we need to recapture a view of life with gratitude.

PART 2
SAY IT!

SAY IT!

"How can I ever thank you?"

A good place to start is by simply saying "thank you." As the sensation of thankfulness begins to fill my being, it's time to identify the source of blessing and let the thanks be heard. Say it loud and clear. Generally, it's appropriate for our thanks to be heard by many. It's good for thanks to be said in the heat of the moment, when the gratitude first starts to burn in our hearts.

Some may struggle with the words or the way to convey gratitude. Fortunately, the scriptures provide guidance with thankful expression, from the Psalmist's recitations to Jesus' prayers and the examples left by folks like Paul. We find that saying thanks has saved people's lives, provided vocation and courage, and enhanced relationships. Saying thanks can even induce sleep.

1

JESUS SAYS THANKS

Lessons concerning thanksgiving come from both Jesus' words and His actions. When did Jesus say thank you? How did He pray His thanks? And how did He express His thankfulness? In revisiting some of our most beloved gospel verses, there is much to learn about gratitude from Jesus. I guess there's no real surprise in that fact; there is always so much to learn from Jesus.

JESUS PRAYS HIS THANKS ALOUD

When the scriptures record Jesus' words of prayer, they are likely to be words of thanks. We know that Jesus often went to a quiet place to pray alone and the content of those prayers is unknown to us. We know, too, how He instructed His disciples to pray, as in the Lord's Prayer. But when we actually "hear" His prayer, we hear Him saying thanks to God:

Thank you for having heard me. (John 11)

Thank you for this cup. (Matthew 26, Mark 14, Luke 22)

Thank you for this bread. (Luke 22)

Thank you for the loaves and fish. (Mark 8, John 6)

From this I understand that it must be important that our prayers of thanks are heard. According to Matthew, when we pray we should to go to our room and shut the door. But Jesus showed us that when we thank God, we should do it publicly. We might ask for forgiveness privately. We might ask for healing in a quiet place. We might look for guidance in prayer when we are alone. But if we have words of thanks to offer God, I think it's good to get out there and say it! Do it! Live it! Let folks know that we thank God for our blessings.

Jesus seems to be following the lessons of the Psalmist who repeatedly instructs us to say our thanks. We are told to sing thanks, play our praise and thanks on loud instruments, make a joyful noise of thanksgiving! And so, Jesus leaves us an example of the significance of praying our thanks to God aloud. If we follow suit, we can turn others' attention to God, the source of so much help, joy, and care.

COURAGE FROM THANKS

Matthew 26:26–28

The thanks that Jesus offered in the upper room are some of the most familiar of all His words. Many congregations retell this story every time they gather for worship. And yet, we may have missed the fact that Jesus offers His thanks in these verses:

"He took the cup and after **giving thanks** He gave it to them, saying, 'Drink from it, all of you; for this is my blood of the covenant, which is poured out for many for the forgiveness of sins.'"

Recently, with a terrific group of thoughtful Christians, I discussed the possible meaning of His thanks in this context. I cannot say with utter certainty what Jesus meant by His thanks—I suppose no one really can. However, in our Bible study we reflected on various possibilities.

It is customary to say thank you for the cup of wine shared in the Passover meal, and Jesus' thanks may have been a part of this custom. It's interesting to note that in Luke's telling of this story, Jesus said thanks for the wine earlier in the meal and then again as He initiated what we now call Holy Communion. Maybe the second thanks was not about the Passover specifically.

As with the spirit of the Thanksgiving holiday, our group considered these words in keeping with the thanks that is shared at the Thanksgiving dinner table. As we do at our annual holiday meal, Jesus may have been expressing his gratitude for the earth's plentiful yield, for the refreshment of the meal's beverage, and for the opportunity to share it with His friends.

With some boldness I suggest that Jesus' thanks meant more than any of these. Is it not possible that Jesus gave thanks to God for what He, Jesus himself, was going to offer all of humanity? Could Jesus have been thanking God for the privilege of being our Savior? Was Jesus declaring His thankfulness in being chosen as the one to sacrifice His life for God's people? "... For this is my blood of the covenant," the new covenant between God and us, and Jesus knew He was the one offering the blood for that new promise.

It's almost painful to imagine our Lord feeling thankful for having to die for us. Why couldn't we just get it right with God, and then Jesus could have been with us into His old age? Could He actually have been thankful for the call to die?

It brings to mind being the president of the United States. Why would anyone want to offer him or herself into a position that draws so much hatred? As president, one knows his life is always threatened and his time is no longer his own. Studies conclude that he will lose years off his life expectancy. Yes, there is a lot of power and respect that comes with the title, but there's also a high price to pay.

And why would anyone want to be a police officer, again facing danger every day? Or a soldier? Or a coal miner? Or a committed parent? Or a devoted teacher?

Please, don't get me wrong. I do not mean to say that such life choices or vocations can truly compare to the sacrifice of our Jesus. And yet, there are many who do choose to give a huge part of themselves for the safety or betterment of others. And lots of these people give thanks for the opportunity to do so! Could this be what Jesus was feeling that night with His closest companions when He knew His death was at hand? After giving thanks, He then told them what He was offering for them—for us. He was our sacrificial lamb and He was thanking God for that.

Just 11 verses later, He asked God to take this cup from Him. The cup of sacrifice and death that He offered in the upper room, He wants to refuse while praying in the garden. But, in the same breath, Jesus acquiesces: "Yet, not what I want but what You want." I believe He was able to say that in prayer because just a few hours earlier He had expressed His gratitude for the cup, for the privilege of being the new covenant. I believe His thanks gave Him courage.

If any of this is anywhere near reality, we find that thanks has yet another amazing side effect. When we acknowledge our thankfulness, it can fortify us with courage when our will is weak. Perhaps it is the underlying thanks that will embolden us to do what is most difficult in life. Saying thanks today for my situation may be what I need to face my tomorrow.

FOR HAVING HEARD ME

"So they took away the stone. And Jesus looked upward and said, 'Father, I thank you for having heard me.'" John 11:41

Isn't it odd that in the prayer Jesus taught His disciples, He never mentioned thanks as a part of that prayer? Why would that be? According to the prayer, found in Matthew and Luke, God's name is to be "hallowed," which may be like saying "Praise God!"—and praise is similar to thanks. But the words, "thank you," are not mentioned in what we have come to call the Lord's Prayer. The Gospel of John does not refer to this prayer but chapter 11 does tell of Jesus praying aloud and giving God thanks. He offers thanks just six verses after He wept. In this very sad time, Jesus gives thanks. In front of God and everybody, Jesus simply prays with thanks that God has heard Him.

Jesus has come into the hometown of His friend, Lazarus, and finds that he is dead and has been lying in a tomb for four days. Lazarus' sisters and others are gathered around the tomb, understandably sad, and now angry that Jesus did not come earlier. If Jesus had come to Bethany when He received word of Lazarus' illness, He may have been able to heal Lazarus, as Jesus had done for so many others. Jesus addresses the situation with a simple prayer of thanks.

There is so much to learn from this thanksgiving prayer of only eight words. One lesson, as we already examined, is the fact that Jesus chose to express this prayer out loud. In this story, Jesus wasn't praying in a lonely place. Here, he prayed aloud in order to be heard by all those mourning at Lazarus' tomb. And in this public prayer, Jesus offered just simple words of thanks to God for hearing His prayer.

These verses are an example of the reoccurring type of prayer I have come to affectionately call the "please and thank you" kind of prayer. It is a prayer petition that is placed before God with utter confidence in God's response. How does Jesus know that His prayer has been heard and answered by God before Lazarus is even seen alive? How can He be so sure that gratitude is in order? Notice Jesus is thanking God first and **then** calling Lazarus out of his tomb. Jesus believes there is cause for thanks before there is evidence. In fact, He is betting His reputation on God's faithfulness by saying these words of thanks aloud in front of the mourning crowd.

Perhaps Jesus didn't know for sure how God would answer His prayer for Lazarus. Jesus says thanks for having **heard** His prayer, and not for having **granted** His wishes. There is a difference. Accompanying Jesus' faith that God hears His prayers is a belief that God will wisely answer prayers. Jesus is trusting God's will in this situation.

It might be said that we learn as much about prayer from these few words as from all of the Lord's Prayer. Let us pray with confidence that our petitions are heard. Let us pray with conviction that we can thank God before the evidence is clear. Let us give thanks for God's wisdom. And, let us pray our thanksgiving aloud that our faithfulness may be a witness to others.

I'LL PRAY FOR YOU

"Two men went up to the temple to pray... The Pharisee, standing by himself, was praying thus, 'God, I thank you that I am not like other people...'" *Luke 18:9–14*

Amy and I heard a song on the radio the other day that caught our attention, made us laugh, and then left us feeling a little sad. The song's title is, "I'll Pray For You" by Jaron and the Long Road to Love. The songwriter leads the listener into his visit to church and his awakening to the significance of prayer, specifically praying for his enemies. And so he begins to pray regularly for his ex-girlfriend. The lyrics sing out his prayer and I'll share some of the words here: "I pray your brakes go out running down a hill, I pray a flowerpot falls from a window sill and knocks you on the head like I'd like to." This isn't the attitude of prayer we are generally accustomed to. Nor is it similar to the prayers we have heard from Jesus.

Sometimes, acts of faithful living become perverted. Jesus witnessed this, as recorded in the Gospel of Luke. There we find the story of a faithful Pharisee dutifully presenting himself to God full of thanks. What could be wrong with that? He is living out his thankfulness, publicly expressing his prayers of gratitude.

Pharisees were faithful people whose whole existence was based on doing everything right. They followed all the rituals, keeping the law perfectly. This was not just their job. This was their life. They were righteous people, for sure. Never having personally met a Pharisee, I base my opinion on the Sunday school stories I was taught along the way. I think in their day, they commanded a great deal of respect among their people. I assume they thought pretty highly of themselves. It's hard not to when you're surrounded by adoring fans and doing the work of Yahweh ,as spelled out in the Torah—which you can recite backward and forward. They were that good.

Now in this story, Jesus is not the one saying thank you, but it tells of a Pharisee who is praying his thanks. Of course, how appropriate that a Pharisee would thank God for who he is. I thank God for who I am, too, so what's all the fuss about that? This Pharisee guy gets it. He's full of thanks and expressing his thanks to God. It's all cool. Why is Jesus so put out by it, making a big fuss of it in this story?

Is it possible to be thankful for the wrong things? Is it possible to be thankful in the wrong way? Apparently so, and Jesus wants us to recognize this. This Pharisee sees himself as better than others, and for that he is thankful. Actually, for that he exalts himself. I can practically hear him calling out: "Hey, God, look at me, look at me. Watch me. I am so good!"

Jesus' stories can be hard to hear when we want to relate to only **some** of the characters. Generally in His stories, we must see at least part of ourselves in **all** of the stories' characters. I learn the most when I place myself within the story from both perspectives. In some ways I am one of the guests, too busy to attend the banquet, in other ways I am called off the street for the banquet. Sometimes I am the lady who lost her coins and sometimes I'm the one invited to her party. I might be the judge or the nagging lady asking for justice. I could be the bridesmaid with the oil for her lamp or the one without! And in this story, I don't want to admit it but I might be the self-righteous Pharisee all hung up on myself and my holy stature, and not just the humble tax collector. I can be thankful for the wrong things, and then even have the nerve to thank God for who I am not!

When we overlook who has helped us achieve what we have achieved in life, we are missing out on cause for thanksgiving. When we ignore the sacrifices of others for our sake and take sole credit for where we are, we've missed another opportunity for thanks. If we cannot give credit where credit is due because we won't even acknowledge the gifts of others, we can't send a thank you note, let alone praise God for those who have lovingly helped us along the way.

The Pharisee in Jesus' parable has another problem, too. Not only has he overlooked the circumstances that have brought him into this position of power, but he has also overlooked the poison of that power. Powerful people can be lauded simply for their power and not their accomplishments—which might even be lacking. Is there anyone around a Pharisee prepared to point out his shortcomings, faults, or errors? Is there anyone who could say to him, "Hey, you're missing your potential"? Is no one there to hold up a mirror for him to see just who he is becoming?

There's at least one more problem for this Pharisee, poor guy. He is looking for personal acclaim by ridiculing others. It's such a childish maneuver, the kind of thing that has been happening throughout history on every playground. I can feel good about myself by claiming my superiority over you. I am king of the hill, and from this post I will declare my worth. My shoes are newer. My parents are richer. My brother is bigger. My bike is faster. My lunch is better. Need I say more?

A perch on this personal pedestal isn't cause for thanks, but rather cause for personal internal examination. The conversation is a reoccurring one in our family, as our teenage kids tell stories of teammates or classmates who always remember their astounding stats, grades, or classroom performance. "Why do you think they need to do that?" we ask our kids. They spit back the answer they know we want to hear: that the bragging students are in need of personal recognition. Maybe those kids hear too many put-downs at home or don't hear anything at and feel ignored. So they make themselves feel good by making others feel bad.

Give God thanks for who you are, not who you are not. Give thanks that you are loving, not more loving than someone else. Thank God for your gifts because they are a blessing in your life, not because your gifts are better than someone else's gifts. And thank God for those who keep you humble and help you refine your faults. Recognize who you are, and be thankful for you. And by the way, I'll pray for you, thanking God for you and the privilege of sharing these thoughts with you.

GRATITUDE INSTEAD OF GRUMBLING

We have considered the prayers of thanks offered by Jesus. In this story, found in chapter 27 of Acts, we find Paul saying his prayers of thankfulness. Although he starts off as an annoying prisoner on a ship, his prayers of thanks save the lives of all those on board. In my opinion, though, Paul starts out on the wrong foot.

I am quickly annoyed by certain personalities, and in those cases may be unwilling to recognize another's gifts and wisdom. Arrogance is an immediate turn-off for me. For instance, if I were a ship's captain, and a passenger—one with no known sailing expertise—tried to give me advice as to when and how to set sail, I would dismiss his comments as pretentious and make mental note to avoid him whenever possible. My disdain would be amplified if the said passenger was a prisoner!

Paul may have evoked such emotion while on the ship in this story from Acts. He had the audacity to tell the sailors that they shouldn't sail due to weather (verse 10). And he did so as nothing more than a **prisoner** being sent to Caesar. In addition to sounding somewhat cocky, those around him may have figured he had an ulterior motive: to avoid arriving in Rome, delay his court hearing, and maybe even finagle an escape. They ignored his warnings. When the northeaster swept down and the ship's crew and passengers faced a very rough storm, Paul made an "I told you so" type of comment (verse 21). Certainly, such an attitude got him no additional respect.

Finally, Paul offered words of thanks to God, encouraging all on board to relax and eat (verses 34, 35), and the crew began to listen to Paul. Is it possible that once Paul expressed his grateful side—his less arrogant self—he then gained the respect of those on board? In this case, giving thanks not only honored God, but it also brought Paul recognition and respect. The story's tone is transformed. The reader can sense the calm assurance that Paul's words brought to those on board. After Paul spoke, they so trusted his words that they ate and placed their confidence in his prediction of imminent safety on land. They even threw the remaining grain overboard, making for smoother sailing toward land they couldn't see, but believed in because of Paul's assurance. And as a result, not one life was lost, even though the ship itself was destroyed.

The sight of a thankful soul in the midst of seemingly unthankful circumstances can call another back to hope. Seeing someone give thanks for the simplest thing, like bread, reminds another of the myriad of causes for thanks in his life. In giving thanks, Paul gave the ship's crew cause to redirect their attention to the possibility that everything would be okay. As they began to act as thankful and hopeful people, their safety drew near. They all reached shore.

Thankfulness is a gift I offer God. I have come to realize that the act of giving thanks is also a gift to me. And now, this story brings to light the fact that others can also be beneficiaries of my public displays of thankfulness. That realization is the easy part. Putting it into action can be much more demanding because looking for appropriate times and places to say thanks can be unsettling. When the general mood is one of doom and gloom, whoa is me, whoa are we, the sky is falling, the sky is falling, it takes a lot of courage to be the one to point out the positive, to see the sunshine, to dare to notice the potential.

One spring, at the start of the baseball season, we spent a huge chunk of a Saturday watching a doubleheader high school game. The games just dragged on and on. The umps were some of the worst. The wind was whipping the field's dry dirt up into our faces. The porta-potty reeked. The players' errors were mounting. We were hungry, and tired, and ready to go home. The air hung with disgruntled remarks. If emotions were clouds, we'd have had a thunderstorm on our hands. And yet, I was feeling really proud of my son and his teammates. And I was happy to be outside enjoying sunshine, a rare commodity in northeast Ohio in early April. And it was nice to be with my family and some of our friends. I smiled internally and tried not to heap more complaints on the fire of disgust we had been feeding. It was another mother who broke the spell saying, "It could be snowing sideways, you know. I'm just glad for the sun I'm getting. Maybe it'll turn into a nice tan!" She lightened the mood, boosted the spectators, and helped us all to start voicing our thanks. The cheering gradually increased and parents found cause for laughter. And hey, we even won the game—finally.

If that kind of thankful comment can alter the heavy mood of disgruntled fans, imagine what power could be unleashed in more significant settings. What if a community began to collect comments of gratitude for their young people and caught them doing good? What if we thanked our elected officials for the good they do, even if they're in a different party? What if we voiced a positive view to the committee that's mired in negativism?

Sometimes when I offer my Pollyanna positive outlook, my words are ignored or minimized. I guess I could quit trying. But adding to the mound of negativity isn't going to do me, or anyone else, any good. So if my words of hopeful thanks are shared or ignored, so be it. At least I'll feel better. And maybe, just maybe, God's promise will be recognized by one other soul because I spoke out. That alone is worth the effort. I'll try to share words of gratitude instead of grumbling.

RECEIVE THE THANKS

"I am grateful to Christ Jesus our Lord, who has strengthened me, because he judged me faithful and appointed me to his service, even though I was formerly a blasphemer, a prosecutor, and a man of violence." I Timothy 1:12–13

Words of thanks are something we all crave. Sounds kind of self-centered, self-righteous, conceited, and immature. But, it's true. At the very least, we want to know that our efforts are appreciated and that someone believes in our potential. Paul's life story is one transformed by Jesus saying, in essence, thank you for who you can become. Is there transforming power in Jesus' thanks for us?

I want my good efforts to be recognized. When an academic project takes all month and is a representation of genuinely good schoolwork, I want the teacher to take note and award an A, because I earned it. When I stop on the road and offer help to a stranded motorist, I hope to at least receive a nod and smile or a quick "thanks."

Do you want your well-developed, good qualities to be recognized? If you know you're a good cook, you want to hear from time-to-time that others appreciate your culinary talents. If the team relies on your ball handling abilities, then you might want to hear that you're doing a great job holding the team together. When your organizational skills led the committee through difficult decisions and did so in a timely manner, a handshake and an attaboy from someone is appreciated—preferably your boss!

You want to be recognized for being the loving, lovable person that you are. You may not always succeed, but you try hard to patiently get daily chores accomplished, without a complaint. Hearing thank you from those you've served makes another day of work more bearable. Days seem to be weekslong sometimes when parenting small children. But a loving hug from your child or thanks from your spouse can fill you with satisfaction, and you try to keep up the good work. Hearing thanks for your smile, thanks for holding the door, thanks for your kind words, all serve as reinforcing gestures for your continued life of loving.

If thanks is not something you crave, let it at least be something you appreciate. When someone voices his appreciation for what you did, who you are, or what you've tried to do, internalize those powerful words. Let another's appreciation energize, excite, empower, or elevate you. You're allowed to be awash in his gratitude for you. To ignore or discount someone's thanks is not only unkind to him, it's unkind to yourself. External evaluations sometimes recognize qualities in you that you didn't acknowledge before—and that can be a good thing.

Paul knew that his hate-filled behavior before he followed Jesus' call was wrong. And yet, Jesus saw within Paul the qualities needed for a world-changing apostle. Even as he tried to tear down the Christian community, Paul was called by Jesus so that his talents could be used in a godly fashion. Jesus judged Paul as one made of faithful desires and in essence said, "Thank you Paul for what you can become, if not for what you are choosing to be right now." Then, the important next step was taken: Paul acknowledged Jesus' appraisal of his ability and he chose to internalize the thanks. Paul became a minister of the Lord because he accepted the praise that Jesus poured down upon him.

We crave thanks. We need thanks. We can be changed by thanks.

Have you ever said, "Thanks for the thank you"? I have. There have been times when the recognition bestowed upon me by others' simple expression of thanks has caught me in my greatest hour of need. For example, once while fretting the low participation in our junior high youth group, I was entering into one of my "let's bash Pam" modes, enumerating all my leadership faux pas. After a disappointing youth meeting, and in the midst of my pity party, I received a phone call from a parent whose teen was in our group. She had called to thank me as the result of a conversation she just had with her daughter. She told her mom, "I want to be more like Mrs. Auble. She's always trying to do nice things for others." The mom just called to thank me for the time I gave to the youth of our community. And like Paul, I felt grateful that they saw something in me that I didn't right then. Their gratitude helped strengthen me for another week of leadership. They helped me acknowledge the fact that I was doing something well, something worthwhile. They were, for me, the voice of Jesus saying, "Thank you for doing my work in the world."

It's vital to daily, happy, and healthy living to give thanks. Likewise, it is vital to daily living to accept thanks when it is poured over us and relish the refreshment that gratitude provides.

8
THANKFUL EXPRESSIONS OF THE PSALMS

The Psalms offer beautiful lessons concerning thankfulness. Here are a few. Let us take joy in publicly expressing our gratitude for God. Remember to thank God whole-heartedly in our victories and courageously in our disappointments. Our life's work will be more meaningful when we live it as an expression of thanks. Make joyful noises and be thankful for the joyful noise of others!

UNCOMFORTABLE THANKS

"Praise the Lords! I will give thanks to the Lord with my whole heart, in the company of the upright, in the congregation." Psalms 111:1

How often do we thank God—in public? I'm not talking about speaking aloud a litany of thanks during worship with a crowd of worshipers, a collective voice. What I am wondering is how often do we say our thanks to God as a single voice in the midst of many?

When the mood is sour and all around us we hear the cursing and raging of the masses about whatever the latest monstrosity might be, this Psalm reminds us that we could be the one positive, dissenting voice. And why? Because not everything is awful. When we look expecting to see God, we will. And when we readjust our expectations, as is sometimes needed, we will see that there is good to be found in most places, in all people, and in many situations.

There are times when complaining leads folks into action and the result is change for the better. However, we have all been in discussions where folks are just flapping their lips with no intention of ever making an effort to change the situation. Those are the times when throwing out words of God's goodness are especially needed.

As can be the case with translations, something is lost when this Psalm is translated into English. Apparently, the author wrote this in the form of an acrostic. It's one of those poems you may have written in second grade, with each line starting with the next letter of the alphabet or letters that spell something special, like "mother," for her big May day. They're fun to do.

Maybe the Psalmist wasn't just having fun, but still, we can learn from the form, as well as the content of this Psalm. In the midst of all that can be so serious and solemn, the writer presents a form that is playful and praiseful. Can we not do the same? When we're bombarded with comments about all that is wrong, all that is broken, all that is neglected, can we take joy in saying that God is good? Can we interject some good that has happened, a success that can be celebrated, some way in which God has been active through God's people?

It's much easier to contribute my complaint about government, or the failure of our schools, or the downfall of our society, or Mrs. Smith's latest social faux pas. Making a comment about something that's gone right can be a conversation stopper, as heads turn to see what that positive statement was meant to infer. And if that comment actually contained God's name—not used in vain—it really puts a halt to the verbal exchange.

Why is that? Have we become a people unable to talk about God's gracious activity in our lives unless we are all seated in the straight-back wooden pews of our sanctuaries? If so, let's get the heads turning, the wheels spinning, and the folks rethinking the plight of the world. Share a word of thanks to God next time you're involved in a downward-spiraling discussion. Let it be a personal challenge to put thankfulness and joy back into conversations involving griping, whining, or general negativity.

What positive word can we offer? In reading the rest of Psalm 111, there are numerous suggestions: God's works are great, full of honor and majesty. God's deeds are wonderful, merciful, and gracious. God provides food. God keeps God's promises. God is just and faithful. God's laws are trustworthy. God has sent redemption. Just pick any one of these and focus on it today. What do these words of the Psalmist mean to you in your present-day world? For example, when I feel like complaining about the coming snowstorm, I can remember that God's works are great, full of honor and majesty. Maybe during the next snowstorm, I can focus on its beauty rather than the inconveniences it will cause. The next step is to boldly interject those praises when I hear my friends fussing about the weather—and then try to smile, too. Am I pushing it a little too much?

Sometimes living a life of thanks requires pushing ourselves, not just a little, but way beyond our comfort zone. I can still be thankful while uncomfortable. I think. Can you?

VICTORIOUS THANKS

Psalms 118

This is a psalm of thanksgiving, perhaps written by a king who has returned, victoriously, from a battle he was not expected to win. Rather than coming before his people puffed up and proud, he comes before God with thanksgiving. In fact, he asks that all the people gathered join him in thanks. He requests permission to enter the temple, not for his own recognition and praise, but rather so that he may thank God.

The scene portrayed by this story reminds me of an interview moments after a game-winning touchdown. Sometimes in those situations, the receiver hails his God and gives all the credit to Jesus Christ, his Lord and Savior. Usually the interviewer glazes over the comment and pushes the star receiver further, asking for comments concerning the offensive line, the quarterback's timely throw into the end zone, and that receiver's amazing catch. The receiver takes the cue and the congratulatory backslapping starts. Thanks to God seems more like a show than a heartfelt psalm.

In this recorded "interview," if the victorious king, the soldiers, the priests, or the people wanted to steal an ounce of credit away from God, there is no evidence of it. Their praise chorus keeps them all on track, with the priests calling the Israelites to offer God thanks and the king recounting God's power as what pulled him through. The gathered follow suit as they sing hymns of exaltation. The priests remind the king that only the righteous may enter the temple, the righteous being those with the right relationship with God. The king wants only to enter the temple so that he and the people of Israel may come before God with thanks. There's not a whole lot of congratulatory back-slapping going on here. It's all God, all the time. "Thanks God. You've pulled out another victory!"

Somewhere in that crowd I bet there was at least one dissenter. There must have been a soldier thinking that his bravery in battle deserved some attention. Wasn't there a priest who thought his fervent prayers contributed to the king's victory? And it's possible that for a fleeting moment, the king saw himself as one of history's best commanders and wanted recognition for that. Wasn't there anyone in that praise-soaked crowd that wanted a word of gratitude directed his or her way? If so, there must also have been another stronger force at work in that place and time. On that day, the faith of the gathered people kept the attention flowing toward God. As one body, they were united in their intent. They kept each other honest and humble. They were gathered there for the purpose of giving God all the glory. The proof is in the first and the last verses of this Psalm. It starts and finishes offering God thanks for He is good and His love will last forever.

As one craves his own recognition or comes to expect thanks, it is good that the faith community reminds him that God is very, very good. And when praise does come his way, it is good that he acknowledges another's gratitude for him, while also vocalizing his appreciation for God's steadfast love and participation. In so doing, he is steered toward humility. And in a state of humility, he may find himself better able to see the value of another, empathize with another, and have compassion for another. A conversation he could have with himself may sound like this: "Yes, I have done well, but so have the others. We are a team. And God has led us here with His great wisdom and understanding."

Thanks can be a tool of evaluation, and therefore critical when assessing one's achievement. Yes, they are thanking me for my performance, but what went well and why did I achieve this success? Who helped me get here? What forces were at work that made this all come together? How can this success be replicated? It wasn't just me who made this happen. Can I identify the elements critical to this success?

Annually, our church supports the efforts of a hunger relief program, CROP, with a walkathon, and in the past I oversaw the planning. The first year went off without a hitch and the congratulatory praises I received were huge. But I knew I'd have to do it all over again the next year. And so, I immediately made sure to recognize all those people who contributed to the event. In reality, they were the ones who deserved the credit. They made the food, put up the signs, made the phone calls, drove where needed, provided care for the event's volunteers, walked the miles, and counted the money raised. I made sure to fully express my thanks for them.

In addition to the people who made the event a success, there were many elements out of our control that worked to our advantage. No one got hurt. The weather was perfect. The volunteers enjoyed being together. In other words, God was very, very good. I don't mean to say that I believe that God cleared the clouds away for us that day, but I do want to recognize that there was a power greater than the sum of the parts and people there that day. I believe that power is God at work in our midst. The Holy Spirit led our efforts. Any one of the individuals participating that day may have failed, but the whole of our efforts—with God as our inspiration—came together and we reached our goal.

At the end of a victorious day, I want to thank God, not me. I hope that those who know me will keep me true to that goal. May we work as a community like the victorious king, the valiant soldier, and the faithful priest who started and finished together with praise and thanks for God.

HANGING ON SO LONG

"Offer to God a sacrifice of thanksgiving, and pay your vows to the Most High. Call on me in the day of trouble; I will deliver you, and you shall glorify me." Psalms 50:14–15

I remember the day it came. The day I received my first rejection letter. They didn't even bother with an envelope, which could have offered my ego a little more protection. They simply sent a post card, open for God and everybody to read. "Thank you for letting us consider this work," hey, at least they said thanks. "Unfortunately, we will not be able to use it in our publishing program." The dream of a published book is not yet accomplished.

I absorbed the rejection and wondered out loud, "So now what?" Of course I knew I needed to try again: a different publisher, a new format, an insider's connection—did I know anybody with that? Every single day I still saw places where thankfulness could transform a situation, where ingratitude was thwarting a person's spirit, or where thanks needed to be said and lived. In those moments I wanted to keep promoting the power of thankful living.

Still, the publisher's rejection called me to review the quality of my material. Some friends and family may have found value in what I wrote. Some were encouraging me to keep on writing. Sometime I was the only one who benefited from my writing. Not knowing day-to-day which scenario it was, I had to struggle to find the courage and drive to keep trying. So why did I? There were several reasons:

1. I write about thanks because I honestly believe this is a place God wants me to be right now. It may not bring about fame, recognition, or any material fortune, but I think God wants me to consider thanks and share what I find.

2. I write about thanks because some folks say they find these thoughts useful, helpful, or inspiring. So, I write about thanks because there may be someone out there who will benefit from these efforts.

3. I write about thanks because **I** need to hear what I write. These words remind me that in every situation there is cause for thanks and a need to live thankfully.

As a substitute teacher I find myself in classrooms littered with teachers' efforts at inspiring students. One attempt included these words plastered on a poster with a kitten dangling from a branch: "When you feel like giving up, remember why you've been hanging on so long." I started this journey choosing steps on a path of conviction; I didn't choose a road toward financial reward. Publishing might bring about the financial affirmation I sometimes crave but that's not why I pursued this call. I have been hanging on because I believe I have wisdom and insight to share, and I believe God has a plan for me to share it.

My daughter offered words of consolation that fateful day of my first publishing rejection. She reminded me that some people will never even receive a rejection letter. Some will never try to submit the book they only dream about. I'm thankful that I tried. And I am grateful for more publishing houses out there, just waiting for the opportunity to send me another rejection letter. And it was touching that my daughter perceived my disappointment. I love her, and I am thankful for her sensitivity.

Thanks in rejection—a few years ago I may not have found cause for thankfulness in such a situation. Now I can say thanks for something even when I'm disappointed. And I hope that others find cause for thanks and a reason to hang on for so long.

AN IMPORTANT JOB TO DO

Psalms 147

When the day is filled with tasks that keep hands and head busy, the exhaustion at the end of the day weighs heavily, like a yoke on the shoulders. There may be a great sense of satisfaction with the day's accomplishments or just the opposite, a frustration that all that needed to be finished was not. And yet, either way the night comes, we close our eyes and rest, preparing for a new day with its to-do list and a hope that the work will be meaningful and lasting.

The Psalmist wants us to comprehend God's activity, not just our own. These ancient words may awaken us to God's tasks and clarify what it is that we must do in response. In Psalm 147 we read that God builds, gathers, heals, binds, determines, gives (three times), understands, covers, prepares, makes, strengthens, blesses, grants, sends, hurls, and declares.

And we are to sing our thanks.

God does everything else. We are to give thanks. That's it. It's our one job and we should do it well.

A neighborhood restaurant provided a venue for our church youth to raise funds for their mission trip, agreeing to donate a portion of the business' profits that evening to the youth group's outreach efforts. Actually, the restaurant staff offered to do all the work if the youth would simply invite folks to dine there that night. Word spread and the place was packed. The youth were on hand to talk with the patrons and answer questions about their mission trip. Some offered to help the staff and Matt was handed a water pitcher and asked to keep water glasses full.

Matt took his job seriously. Repeatedly, he walked from table to table and asked guests if they wanted more water, filling countless glasses and refreshing the guests. Several times, he refilled his water pitcher and in so doing became comfortable behind the counter at the water sink. Sometimes guests were seated and had no water glass yet, so Matt took it upon himself to get them a glass from behind the counter so he could fill it, because filling water glasses was his job. The stack of clean glasses ran out and Matt asked how to wash them, was shown how, and added that to his charge so he could have clean glasses to fill. Then he started to clear the tables and retrieve those dirty glasses, wash them, set them at a diner's place and then keep them filled. He had just one responsibility: to keep the water glasses full, and he fulfilled his obligation. In so doing, he was bussing tables, washing dishes, and filling water glasses.

Sometimes in order to do one job well, we have to take on more responsibility.

If we are going to abide by Psalm 147 and take our thanking job seriously, we will have to take on more responsibility, like Matt. Matt had to figure out how to fill the pitcher, wash the dishes, and clear the tables, just so he could fill the glasses. Similarly, if we are going to sing our praise, the piano better be in tune, and we should know the music we are singing well. If we plan on writing our thanks, the pencil should be sharpened and plans for publishing our thanks need to be in order. If we want to proclaim our thanks, the microphone needs to be in good working order so our thanks can be heard and a crowd of listeners needs to be invited for an audience. If we are going to live our thanks, our lives must be ordered in a way that expresses our thanks. Yes, we have only this one charge, to "sing to the Lord with thanksgiving" (verse 8), but performing this needed task could be a lifelong endeavor.

When we are tending to our job of giving thanks, we are always looking for reasons to be thankful. We notice that God is healing. God is binding. God is giving. God is blessing. God is declaring. And we are thanking God by giving, too. In giving thanks, we shift the attention from ourselves and onto God and God's people. We thank God by healing. We thank God by declaring God's love. And we thank God by trying to be a blessing. We behold God's goodness, we discern our call to sing thanks to God, and we discover a fitting way to express our thanks. That's our job.

Yet, giving thanks is more than a job. It's an opportunity, an invitation to give to God so that our living is more full, more abundant. Returning to Matt's story, he didn't work at the restaurant; he was not employed there. Filling water glasses wasn't really his job; it was an opportunity he chose to pursue. That opportunity filled his hours that evening with purpose and gave him a means to genuinely contribute to the workings of the restaurant. Matt made others' visit there more comfortable.

The opportunity we have before us as people of faith is to recognize God's activity and give thanks. Our hands and heads will be busy every day with actions that express thanks. Our activity is sure to be meaningful when the purpose is to give God thanks.

JOYFUL NOISE

"Make a joyful noise to the Lord, all the earth... Enter God's court's with thanksgiving, and into God's courts with praise." Psalms 100:1, 4 (Oh, just go and read the whole Psalm. It's wonderful!)

In your life, what are the joyful noises?

"AWE, ACE!" is a joyful noise. That's Amy's volleyball team celebrating another point. When the server hits the ball over the net and the opposing team isn't able to hit it back, it's called an ace serve. Sometimes the serve is so hard, fast, and amazing, it looks as if the other team is in awe, simply watching a thing of beauty sail over the net, forgetting it's the game ball that needs to be returned with three bumps over the net. They watch it fall to the floor and our team gets a point. Our team cheers together, "awe ace!" Then the opposing team wakes up and realizes they need to return that ball if they want to stay in the game. Our girls are a hard working team of 14-year-olds who support each other and revel in their victories. They laugh a lot, and that's another joyful sound.

For me, the sound of the front door opening and closing is another joyful noise. It means a family member has returned home from somewhere. He or she is safe and we can spend some time together. With a young teen driver and a traveling husband, that door sound is a joyous answer to a prayer.

Centerpeace is a joyful noise, or shall I say they make joyful music. It's a small group of faithful church members who sing for our worship and other special events. Their faith radiates from their voices and faces as the congregation absorbs the message of their music and their lives.

What a joyful noise to hear playful sounds of the nine children under the age of nine who live in the two houses across the street from us! Seriously, with windows open I relish the laughter, conversation, and occasional bickering of these wonderful, little neighbors who inject the air with sounds of life.

One more. I love the joyful noise of the frogs, crickets, and birds that constantly fill the air with their calls and music most of year. In a public park, field, or my wooded back yard, I find these creatures in God's world calling out their praises. It's as if they are singing tribute for the gift of another day. Be it sunny and dry or wet and chilly, they are faithful to their duty and it's a joyful noise I crave.

What type of joyful noise did the Psalmist foresee when writing Psalm 100? When asking for us to "make a joyful noise to the Lord" and "enter the gates with thanksgiving" did the Psalmist beckon for opening and shutting doors, cheering teams, strumming guitars, shouting children, and croaking frogs? In Psalm 150, praise is called for in the form of trumpets, cymbals, tambourine, dance, pipe, and string. Why not with all other manner of joyful living?

Thankful people make joyful noises. Thankful people hear joy declared throughout God's creation. Whether it be clanging cymbals or clapping hands, a rendition of thanks lie within the noise. Tambourine or tap dance can proclaim our joyful thanks to God. Let joyful noises be made in our articulation of praise and in our recognition of another's expression of praise. I believe that a life of faith produces and perceives sounds of appreciative living.

While struggling through the '70s as a child, I found new ways of living joyful noise for God with my church youth group and youth minister, Gil Hubbard. He encouraged me to play guitar in worship for the first time. Also under his guidance, our youth group prepared and presented a service of worship unlike any I had ever witnessed. Among other things, we actually adorned the chancel with helium balloons—now that's a joyful expression if you've ever seen one! Well, that's what we thought. Apparently, a few established church members found it offensive, especially when some balloons let loose and floated into the sanctuary rafters, some 100 feet high. Those angry folks couldn't hear the joy in our thanksgiving; they only heard riotous voices of youth ignoring the sanctity of holy worship. Oops.

I give credit to Gil and the senior minister who had to calm the angry elders of the church. Our pastors never let on that there were angry adults who heard no joy in our youthful praise and saw balloons as an inappropriate means of thanks. Our youth group continued to prepare and present worship at least twice a year, not always with balloons, but consistently with unorthodox means of joyful and thankful pronouncement. It was not until 15 years later that I found out some opposed our youth-led worship because, in the spirit of the Psalmist, Gil had continued to encourage our personal acclamations of joyful praise.

With eyes and ears tuned into the potential, praise can be found in unexpected realms and thanks may be sung in unusual tones. Therefore, seeing it requires intention. Hearing it demands an open spirit. I don't want to miss out on an opportunity to be excited, happy, or thankful, so I guess I better be willing to see praise potential in a variety of expressions.

Let us go out today and listen for noise that induces a smile, sound that fills us with thanks, clamor that recalls for us God's gifts. We can make joyful noises and enter into God's gates with thanksgiving, into God's courts with praise to give thanks to God and bless His name. We can find cause to yell out, "AAAAWWWWE ACE!"

9
SPECIAL THANKS ON SPECIAL DAYS

Say it now! An ordinary day is made into a special day when thanks are spoken. Don't wait for a special occasion. No need to hold off until you can write a formal thank-you letter. When the spirit moves, and there's reason for thanks, say thank you! As my friend Elizabeth said, "Many of us must have fleeting feelings of gratitude and appreciation, but then we rush on with life." So say thanks now.

PERFECT TEENS (BIRTHDAYS)

"How can we thank God enough for you in return for all the joy that we feel before our God because of you?" I Thessalonians 3:6–10

We have two November babies. Well, they were babies years ago. Now they are teens—and you know what they say about teenagers. Yet, my husband and I still find cause to celebrate their birthdays and find ourselves feeling pretty grateful for them. In fact, we find reason to celebrate those two almost every day, not just on their birthdays.

When I talk with people about my kids, sometimes I'm a little embarrassed. They are such wonderful people and it seems that everything I say is perceived as bragging, selective memory, or simply parental ignorance of the facts. With two teens it's supposed to be a very tough time, and it may become difficult tomorrow, but today, they are just great. They are kind, hardworking, determined, funny, smart, and just plain cute, even at 14 and 17.

Without a doubt, there are those who would argue with my assessment. A few of Andy's teammates and friends are probably tired of his cross comments when, in his opinion, they're not working hard enough. Amy has high standards of friends and can seem standoff-ish with some. I am sure others from their schools could tell us things about them I may not want to hear. But then, character is judged by standards as varied as the weather.

I find myself feeling like Paul in his first letter to the Thessalonians, not knowing how to fully thank God for all the joy brought to me by my children. The good news of their faith and love consume my heart, and any expressions of thanks seem inadequate. And yet, how good it is that I have put this in writing because I am sure there will be times, probably within the next 24 hours, that I am going to forget all the goodwill I'm feeling right now!

A vital part of feeling thankful is recognizing thankworthy times when we are experiencing them. A crucial part of expressing thanks is seizing the opportunity **now**! In parenting circles, its called "catching them doing good." Instead of trying to watch for every error or infraction, parents need to watch diligently for children doing the right thing. Catch your son getting home before curfew. Notice your daughter hasn't been on the computer at all today. Appreciate the times that they do a fine job raking the leaves. Notice the times when they don't argue with your requests. And then tell them "thank you."

I have to admit this is still a work in progress for me. There are days when I expect their failure, and I find it. I'll be frantically trying to pick up around the house and only see the stuff my kids didn't put away. If I'm careful to hold off on my tirade, I'll notice their genuine efforts: Amy's been emptying the dishwasher and Andy is finishing his homework. Maybe they left their school books sprawled over the living room floor, but at least it's because they were studying or cleaning up the dishes.

Beyond the interactions with my children, I need to look for others doing the best they can and catch them doing good, as well. When watching the ref make one bad call after another, I feel my heart rate soar until I allow myself to see the foot fault he missed by our volleyball player. And yes, that cashier is really slow, but she's actually talking to customers and treating us like humans. It takes time to actually interact with customers and that's a good thing to try to do.

Although I may not feel the overwhelming joy for the ref or the clerk that I feel for my beloved children, all these situations bring to light the same principle: if we are looking for them, we will find ample causes for giving thanks daily. There are people who make life better, easier, more loving, more worthwhile, funnier, meaningful, purposeful, and happier. Catch someone doing something right today and then thank him. At the very least, thank God for that person today. And next time you find yourself wishing someone a happy birthday, be sure to mention how thankful you are for him.

TREAT BAGS WIDE OPEN FOR MORE (HALLOWEEN)

"Devote yourselves to prayer, keeping alert in it with thanksgiving… Let your speech always be gracious…" Colossians 4:2, 6

Our little community experiences an annual invasion each year on Halloween when more small children than I can count fill the streets. Our family welcomes the costumed visitors in our garage—we move the car out and replace it with folding chairs. Ancient cardboard bats and black cats hang from the ceiling. The paper towel ghosts made by our once-small children adorn a garage shelf, illuminated by the flickering light of the carved pumpkins. One by one costumed children parade into the garage with bags open wide. Most of them chant the Halloween ritual, "trick-o-treat," and many remember to say thank you. One year a particularly small fairy princess walked up to me with no words what so ever. She stood gazing at me and I at her. I gave her two suckers and she didn't move. Her mother offered the necessary prompt, "What do you say, Cassie?" The angelic princess responded, "please" without flinching and stood waiting for more. Cassie's mom, now an embarrassed parent, grasped Cassie's hand and marched her back out to the street and to another home.

The whole thing made me laugh and got me thinking about—what else—thanks.

We come parading before God with our prayer requests and the needs of the world heavy on our hearts. We fall to our knees with treat bags wide open and await answered prayers like treats from God. As the bag grows heavy with one sweet treat after another we still hold the bag open and await more. Our mothers would remind us to say thank you, to **be** thankful, but we forget ourselves and our manners and just keep asking for more, saying "please."

Paul asks us to be alert to thanksgiving in our prayer and gracious in our speech. In other words, with both God and people, we need to share our thankful hearts. Yes, we can ask for what we need from God and from others, but it sounds as if Paul wants us to first be aware of what we have, to distinguish our wants and wishes from our needs. Take note and live with thanks for prayers already heard and answered. Likewise, graciously recognize the efforts of others who have done their best for us.

I have at least one more Halloween analogy: As children on the special night, my brothers and I would run from one house to another, wanting to fill our bags to the brim. Then we'd come home, dump the treats on the floor of the living room, and start surveying each other's haul. Soon after, the trading began, as if each piece of candy was a valuable commodity in the stock market. We'd eat until we were sick, go to bed, and get up in the morning and start gorging ourselves again. After the third day or so, the Halloween candy would become less attractive. By the end of the week, my mom could have thrown away what was left over and we wouldn't have even noticed. What we had to have, had to have more of, and had to trade to have just the right amount of, was now unwanted. We thought we'd wanted it and would be more happy if we had more of it. Sometimes, we find that having less of it—whatever it may be—is plenty to be thankful for.

Even if Halloween is months away, today let's make every effort to recognize how full our trick-o-treat bag already is and try to say thank you rather than please.

51 THANKS! (MORE BIRTHDAYS)

"We always give thanks to God for all of you and mention you in our prayers, constantly remembering before God your work of faith and labor of love and steadfastness of hope in our Lord Jesus Christ." I Thessalonians 1:2–3

Birthday celebrations vary from one household to another. I discovered this when I married Dave and we began celebrating our birthdays and then those of our children. He asked why I had to make such a big deal out of his or our kid's birthdays. I was shocked! What else is there to do but make a big deal—it's your birthday for goodness sake! It's the one day a year when we celebrate just that one person, the birthday girl or boy! He eventually bought into my way of seeing things, and so we have cake and gifts and a special meal of the birthday person's choosing. The gifts don't have to be expensive, just thoughtfully selected for the recipient.

Last year, on my special day, when I was the birthday girl, my family returned the favor and made my day very special. Actually, they made it a great week, with birthday meals, gifts, special cards, and foods. I felt awash with their love and overwhelmed with thanks. I actually wrote out a list of gratitude gifts: presents that come without wrappings, but wrap me up with joy! For me, it'll become an annual tradition. Here's what I wrote:

Today, on my fifty-first birthday, I offer these 51 thanks. I am thankful for…

Ministers in my life: Gil, Bob, Norm, Ken, Chad, Dick and Sue, Judy, and my Mom, who stood with me on the day I was consecrated as a diaconal minister…

The pink and golden sky at the east end of Hinsdale Drive this morning; the carpet of gold and red leaves on the street; the promise of warmth today; lunch today with a long-ago friend; my daughter's sleepy greeting "happy birthday, mom;" Dairy Queen birthday cakes; Charles Schultz and the entire Peanuts gang…

My Dad's love for life and for my children; my son's love for his grand-parents; two brothers who taught me the art of argument, although they still always win; my grandmothers and great-grandmothers, who raised wonderful children who eventually raised me; my husband who some-how manages to love me everyday…

President Obama's courage; dentists who are kind and gentle; neighbors who have wonderful humor for life and lots of cool children; the green door across the street and where it leads when I open it; garbage men who smile when they work…

Dark chocolate M&M's; family time to watch M*A*S*H together; 246 unique hits on my blog; the 1,632 times that someone has visited my site; Monroe's Orchard, just 2 miles from our home, and their autumn pears; my friend Chris and his courage to do the right things...

The dobro and Bob playing it; the banjo and Emliss playing it; the mandolin and Dale playing it; the saxophone and Roy playing it; the harmonica and Jerry playing it; the piano and Amy playing it; the music of James Taylor, Taylor Swift, Alison Krause, and Claire Lynch...

Paul's letter to the Roman's and the Philippians; the Gospel of John; Micah; Sunday School teachers, youth group leaders, and seminary professors who were more interested in getting me to think about my faith than they were in telling me the answers; my parents' positive view of life; my dad's recitations of the saying, "If you don't have anything nice to say, don't say anything at all," and the fact that I remember that more clearly than the off-color jokes he was yelled at for telling us as kids...

Warm slippers; dry shoes; back handsprings that I used to be able to do repeatedly; windy days; pink granite rock shores of Georgian Bay, Ontario; a clean house, or a messy house filled with those we love.

As birthdays roll around for those you love, do what you can to let them know how thankful you are for them. And as your birthday comes, I invite you to mention in prayer or meditation a long list of thanks, one that goes beyond the obvious and may dig into the roots of your firm grip on joyful living! Try to mention one thanks for every year you've lived, because the older we become, the more opportunities we've had to rack up the gratitude gifts.

JOY! (ADVENT AND CHRISTMAS)

Luke 2 and Matthew 2

He just sat there in the seat of the car, with a cell phone to his ear and me listening to him crow. I hadn't seen a smile that deeply embedded in his face for weeks. "Awesome, dude!" Pause. "Awesome! That's so awesome!" Another pause for listening. "It's so awesome! Dude, that's awesome!" I could continue to share that dialogue here, but the same words are simply repeated for the next five minutes.

Shear joy! The news found my friend overwhelmed with all-consuming joy! His father would be moving back to Ohio, having been offered a new job. The expectation of having his family together again encircled him with hope, peace, joy, and love—amazing how all four of those come together at life altering moments. My friend now had cause for hoping that his family would be reunited and so much of his life would be put back in order. There was a sense of peace for him that his dad was employable, desired the work, and wanted to lead their family in a good way again. And of course, there was the simplicity of joy, of having cause for celebration and thanksgiving. Overriding all of this is love, the kind of love that develops within a family, from shared history and care for each other.

When the phone call ended, joy made my friend almost speechless. He was able to basically say just one word: "Awesome!" Then, as the joy settled into his being, he finally closed his cell phone, sat still as he recovered, and then exploded. He blossomed with enthusiasm as he told me of all the new possibilities. His joy was uncontainable. He found himself overflowing with words, unable to stop talking and get out of the car when we reached our destination.

When we are overcome with happy thankfulness, it's called joy!

Christmas joy can be like this. There are moments almost every year when the implications of this story strike me with sheer joyful force. Instead of babbling with repeated choruses of "awesome," I usually cry. Tears of joy leave me speechless. Then, I find myself wanting to explain my revelation. I want to tell anyone who might listen what an amazing story this Christmas delivers.

This joyful experience may be similar to that of the shepherds, stunned into silence by the angels' revelation, and then later running the streets of Bethlehem blabbing the incredible story. Mary, too, was silent in her joy, pondering the unusual events. In Matthew's account, there is no dialogue recorded when the Magi met the Infant King—the scripture simply says "they were overwhelmed with joy." We do not know if or how they later shared the magnificent details of their travels of homage.

Let us consider at this point that a significant part of Christmas joy is allowing ourselves to be consumed by it. Let our souls shout "awesome" as we permit the joy to permeate our somewhat tough skins.

Let us also consider that the joy of Christmas can be, and ought to be, shared with wild expression, nearly unrestrainable chatter, or concentrated effort. The joy of our faithful discovery, or re-discovery, is worthy of sharing.

We must allow ourselves time to be consumed by joy. We must allow ourselves time to share that joy. My Christmas wish for you this day is that you give yourself the time to bask in Christmas joy!

Merry Christmas my friends!

SANTA LEFT (EPIPHANY, OR THE DAYS AFTER CHRISTMAS)

The throne is empty. There is no line of anxious and excited children. The camera and photographer-turned-elf is gone. This part of the bustling mall is now deserted. There is no Santa in the house.

As I gazed at the late December scene, I was inspired. What if Santa stayed in his seat of honor through the New Year and children came to sit on his lap just to say thank you—you had to see that coming from me. It would be such an amazing life lesson for our children and families. Maybe some kids would bring handmade thank-you letters. Others might show Santa pictures of themselves hugging their Christmas puppy, or sitting on their new bike, or wearing their new winter clothes. Some would be overcome with joy and hug Santa's neck, burying their smiling faces in his beard. Now there's a photo-op the elf won't want to miss!

Inviting Santa to stay with us for an extra week might encourage us to slow down and enjoy the day we've prepared for and awaited for over a month! Rather than hurrying to get the Christmas tree cleaned up, the fattening food put away, and the outdoor lights taken down, we might make a special effort to reflect on the glory of the day and say, "Thank you, Santa." Heck, we might even remember to say thanks to Mary for being willing to trust God. Thank you, shepherds, for overcoming your fear. And thank you, wise men, for going out of your way to meet the foretold King. And by the way, thank you, God, for the gift of Your love and of Your Son who taught us how to love.

On the last day of their Christmas vacation, my kids took time to write thank-you notes to family and friends who gave them gifts this Christmas. Okay, I had to remind them repeatedly to do this, but they did. And the letters were thoughtful and kind. A few times my daughter had to stop and jog her memory, "What did Aunt Jody get me this year?" Embarrassment would flood her face as she recalled the gift she received that she simply couldn't get off her mind two weeks ago, the thing she really, really wanted for Christmas this year.

Her experience is not unique to her. I know through my lifetime I have done the same. The things I most urgently longed for, and then received, I now take for granted. I wanted to graduate from school so I could finally work in the world. I wanted to be married to a loving man. I wanted to be a mother. I wanted to own a comfortable home. I wanted to share my talents and abilities with a congregation. I want… I want… I want. And then, I receive… I receive… I receive. And sometimes before I even had time to settle into a life of thanks, I found myself saying again: I want… I want… I want. It's as if Santa just up and left for the North Pole and I never even got to say thank you.

That's the amazing thing about faithful thanks. We don't have to hold off until God comes back around to say thanks. We don't have to wait in line at the mall. We don't even have to get out our stamps, pens, and thank-you notes. However, we do have to set aside the time to relish our thankfulness. We need to slow down—no **stop**—and be thankful. Say a prayer of thanks. Write it down, if that helps. Breathe in with gratitude. Exhale with joy. Count our blessings. Bury our happy faces in God's white beard (if I can borrow a stereotypical portrait of God just to make a point) and hug Him around the neck, sitting on His lap and expressing our overwhelming thanks.

Take a pointer from Paul. No less than nine letters in the New Testament include words of thanks within the first chapter. This says to me that Paul realized the significance of recognizing cause for thanks. And he didn't keep those joyful thoughts to himself. He clearly stated his appreciation to God for those in Rome, Corinth, and Thessalonica, to name a few. Paul said thanks.

As with my children, may I remind you to write a few Christmas thank-you notes? If Christmas is long gone, there is still cause for writing thanks: a dinner invitation, a birthday present, an act of kindness. Remember that cause and write a note. Then, take it a step further. Recall what you are utterly grateful for—the gifts without wrappings or warranties. Say your thanks to God and live your thanks with God's people. And thus, be happy in the New Year.

THANKS FOR MLK AND OTHER PROPHETS

Martin Luther King, Jr. was an amazing prophet of our times. On the day of his remembrance, we are called to honor his life with thanks. We can thank God for MLK. We might learn more about MLK and come to know of his courage. We can speak our thanks for this man and the efforts of acceptance he worked for. We can live our thanks by volunteering our time as a part of the MLK Day of Service, which has become a regular part of this annual celebration.

As an expansion of that day's celebration, consider those who have inspired you to be a loving, accepting, and caring person. Think of someone who has driven you to a higher potential. Recall the prophetic voice that may have called you into service, ministry, or a selfless vocation? Name this person of courage in your life. In recognition of Martin Luther King, Jr., write a letter of thanks to a prophet in your life. I have done the same.

Our efforts will require us to identify not only the person, but also his or her gifts that have inspired us. Putting our thanks in writing can solidify that vague feeling we have of respect for someone we remember making an impression on us. As we search for the words to convey thanks, we can take pleasure in recalling that person's affect on us. In sending along these words of thanks, we may encourage the one who once encouraged us. Our thanks may inspire that prophet to continue his or her good works in the lives of others. Our note may simply make that person smile and give him or her joy in the day. In other words, writing a thank-you note is a gift for the one writing it, as well as the recipient. And in this case, this thank you can be an act of our thanks to Dr. King.

10
TRANSFORMED BY THANKS

Expressing thanks has a transformative power, for the one receiving the thanks as well as the one testifying thanks.

THANKS ON THE RUN

"Don't worry about anything, but in all your prayers ask God for what you need, always asking Him with a thankful heart. And God's peace, which is far beyond human understanding, will keep your hearts and minds safe in Christ Jesus." Philippians 4:6–7 (TEV)

Sometimes praying for me is like running in circles, and that's a good thing! I keep coming back to "thank you, God," often followed by "please help, God." And that circle of thanks and please repeats itself over and over, like running laps on a prayer track. It's similar to the instructions given to the faithful in Philippi.

The author of Philippians, in chapter 4, instructs that when we come before God with words of petition, when we ask God for what we need, we must do so with a thankful heart. The writer here is like the parent of a young child, reminding him to say please and thank you—at the same time. In other words, when we come to God in prayer we come with faith, too, faith that God will hear our prayer and will respond. God will answer our prayer. There is overwhelming thankfulness in that realization. Deep trust in our God's faithfulness results in prayers that simultaneously ask for and thank for what we need.

Our overwhelming needs sometimes bring us into God's presence with overwhelming worry. It's a time when we have to stop and recall all that God has already done for us. Remembering the prayers God answered in the past, and recounting the blessings we've already been given, brings us out of worry and into thanks. Our hearts are full of thanks, not only for the prayers that God is going to answer, but also for all that God has already supplied. I have found that for me, prayers of thanks are my place to start every conversation with God.

In the cold winter months of life in Northeast Ohio, I have a retreat that calls my heart to thanks and my restless body to exercise. The local college indoor track has become a prayer sanctuary for me. The air is warm and welcoming—even in the sub-zero weather. It's usually quiet, even if others invade my private haven. The large windows overlook a white-blanketed soccer field, gentle hills, and outdoor track decorated with paths left by brave souls walking, skiing, or sledding. In the distance, the dark trees, in their winter attire, encircle the area, sometimes filtering the sunlight, the moonlight, or the early morning dawn glow. It is here that I meet my Maker.

Literally running circles, while trying to keep track of miles, used to cause me consternation and disrupted my otherwise fulfilling endeavor. But I have discovered a new way of counting laps. With intentional effort, I use each lap as time for prayer with God. If I am planning to run 20 laps, I come to God with prayers of praise and thanksgiving for the first 10. I search my heart for all that brings joy, order, comfort, safety, and health to my life and the lives of others. The second 10 laps are dedicated to prayers of petition, as I humbly consider my needs, the help our community requests, or the comfort our world requires.

Honestly, my prayer life has not been one of great note or regularity. Being a person who can barely sit still for any length of time, trying to be at rest while sharing time with God in prayer has been tough and generally unrewarding. I find my mind wondering over my to-do lists, or reviewing memories, or lapsing into light sleep. The greatest success I've had has been in journaling my prayers, a practice that filled boxes with used spiral notebooks and scared me with the chance that my private life may be discovered by uninvited eyes.

Jogging my prayer time has finally matched my spiritual hunger with my physical design, so now my prayer time is met with never before experienced joy and longing. And, it has increased my awareness of my blessings. Starting every run with lap after lap after lap of thanksgiving has found me bringing to God praise for aspects of my life and this world that I have not stopped to realize before: the subtleties of the changing weather, the countless people whose work enhances our days, the personality traits that endear my family members to me, the benefits of a civilized society, the compassion of neighbors, the gifts of strangers, and the presence of God. I never lack new subjects of gratefulness.

The fact that at least half of my time in prayer is dedicated to only thanks and praise seems fitting and appropriate for my personality. Away from my prayer track, I can find fault with too many aspects of daily living. Taking time to count my blessings, as I count my laps toward another mile, balances my day and more importantly, refocuses my attentions. When I leave the gym, I am more likely to connect with all that is good in my day and continue in an attitude of thankfulness.

When a new lap begins and words of praise do not quickly jump to my heart, the lap may be dedicated to silent listening. God's activity with me is acknowledged and God reminds me of a forgotten blessing or unnoticed gift. These laps of listening help remold my heart into a Philippians-style thankful heart.

When they were younger, my son and his friends would occasionally accompany me to the gym, where their activity moved them on the basketball court directly underneath the raised track. The boys had to gather their equipment and get permission from parents. I played chauffeur and drove around town collecting young ball players. Coordinating our schedules brought me to the track one afternoon at an unexpected time and in a frazzled state of mind. My jog began with one foot in front of another, barely aware of what I was doing, still reeling from what they were doing and how we were getting it all together. Ten steps into the ritual, my reality crashed over my head. I could pray now! This was **my** time now, just me and God. The first laps were simply thanks for being able to be in God's presence as I came to feel the enormity of this privilege and my joy in realizing it. I became aware of a gaiety I never recalled feeling so intensely about the prospect of prayer time with God! My concept of prayer had completely shifted from duty to delight.

Opening every prayer run with laps of thanks has transformed my relationship with **life**. When I start by first recalling causes for thanks, I am led into a better position for petitions because I am more fully aware of the distinction between needs and wants. Opening prayers with thanks brings to mind the answered prayers God has attended to already. I start my conversation with God with a thankful heart. In all honesty, however, my thankful attitude fails me from time to time. When I leave the track, there are days, or nights, when I forget to practice what I preach and pray... and I miss out on a good night's sleep.

SLEEP IS A GOOD THING

More on Philippians 4:6–8

It was a long night for me. I woke up in the wee hours of the night and could not get back to sleep. My mind was racing over all the activity of the Thanksgiving weekend and zooming ahead through the load of extra action items of the Christmas season. I fretted over health concerns of loved ones and frantic schedules of my children. I mulled over plans for the new day and upcoming week, as well as an ever-growing to-do list.

Other such times I lie awake and pray through the sleeplessness. I say prayers of thanks and petitions of concern. My prayers calm me and lull me back to sleep. That night, however, my busy mind would have none of it. There was simply too much worrying to do and no time for sleep. The next morning, in my drowsy state, I was angry that I would not allow myself to let it all go. There may be a time for worry, but there is also a time for succumbing to the presence and peace of God. And there is a time for sleep! As we know from Philippians 4, thanks is a way to whittle away at worry and put God back in God's place.

Paul is asking the Philippians to consider putting please and thank you in the same breath. Their reward? Peace of mind and no worries. If we follow Paul's instruction, we will take to God, in prayer, all our needs. Place those needs before God and simultaneously, thank God for helping us through it all. Expect God's participation in our lives and then expect God's peace to fill us.

This is not to say that with such a prayer we will find ourselves living a trouble-free life. Paul specifically says to ask for what we **need** and we will find **peace**. He did not say pray for all we **want** and all our wishes will come true. I am sorry if this reads like the small print found at the bottom of all those holiday store coupons, with restrictions and limits, leaving the shopper feeling misled. Recognize that Paul is promising an internal stillness when we learn to ask and then let go. We are able to let go because of the unfaltering faith that assures us that God will walk us through whatever we will face. Such a deep faith expresses itself as thankfulness. And so, we pray with thanks.

I pray for safety, and give thanks that God will accompany me through difficult passage. I pray for health, with a thankful heart that God will heal my spirit. I pray for my community, and give thanks knowing that I can serve as God's hands for my neighbors. I pray for comfort, and my thankful heart sings in the knowledge that God abides with me. I pray. I give thanks. I find peace. I overcome my worries.

So where was all that peace at three in the morning?

Truth be told, I am a fraud. I write what I need to hear, reminding myself of the lessons I have learned and need to relearn. At least by putting these lessons in writing, there is a possibility that you and I can come to a better place together. Maybe the next time I find myself sleepless and full of worry, I'll remember what I wrote and will listen to our lesson and find the peace I hoped to share with you. Perhaps I'll start with please, God; thank you, God; peace from God. And maybe, I'll find sleep again.

365 THANK YOUS

When Valentine's Day rolls around, do you find yourself still needing to finish your Christmas thank-you notes? Is February too late to send them out? We know that a handwritten note is going to mean so much more than a cyber note—it's worth the 40-some cents in postage. The recipient may even keep that note of thanks and post in on the fridge or put it in a special place. Maybe our efforts will inspire the recipients to send out a thank you note themselves. I love the potential multiplying effect of thanks!

Not to be overlooked is the transformative power of thanks on the one expressing gratitude. Making an effort to recognize what we are thankful for and why a gift means something to us causes us to focus on the joy of receiving a gift. According to lawyer John Kralik, the act of daily gratitude can change a life—it changed him!

365 Thank Yous is the book Kralik wrote about his year of writing thank-you notes every day—starting with his Christmas gift thank yous. As the New Year dawned on Kralik, his future was dim and he was depressed. As he wrote the daily notes though, he witnessed his own metamorphasis. He found that even if his actual situations didn't always improve, his attitude did. Furthermore, he found that expressing his thanks did change others' actions and opinion of him. Things in his life eventually began to look up. He spoke about his book and his experience with Liane Hansen on NPR's *Weekend Edition* (December 26, 2010), and I was inspired, again, on my crusade for thanks. The interview and his book confirmed my suspicions that thanks, seen and spoken, changes people.

The NPR website lists 10 tips for writing the perfect thank you note, all from author John Kralik. I invite you to read his suggestions. Kralik has some very good, original points: Keep it short. Think about the person whom you are writing to and what they went through to gift you. Be mindful of the gift's potential for you. Read on at www.npr.org/2010/12/26/132263637/perfect-thank-you-notes-heartfelt-and-handwritten

In Luke, the healed Samaritan publicly threw himself on the ground at Jesus' feet as a way of expressing his heartfelt gratitude. In comparison to that, writing a little heartfelt note seems easy. Either way, we just have to make sure we do it.

THANKS FROM A FOREIGNER

"Then one of them, when he saw that he was healed, turned back, praising God with a loud voice. He prostrated himself at Jesus' feet and thanked him. And he was a Samaritan." Luke 17:11–19

The story of the 10 lepers who are made clean by Jesus is such a wonderful children's story because it clearly paints the beauty of saying thank you. Ten receive Jesus' gift of healing. One sends a thank-you note. Actually, he shows up in person to say his thanks to Jesus, face-to-face. Of course, the others may be back home hugging their children, recounting the story to their parents, joyfully reuniting with their friends. But this one makes the effort to find Jesus and praise God at His feet with a loud voice! The healed Samaritan's thanks are visibly sincere. It's an appropriate example for our young children who need to learn the value of saying thank you.

Maybe the Samaritan came back to thank the Healer because he, of the 10, was the most surprised. He was the one healed in a foreign land. It's like receiving health care at no cost when you break your arm during your visit to Canada. There's no paperwork to fill out, no charge for the prescription (as long as you can get back over the border with it), no required follow-up visits with more co-pays to cover. This is an unexpected privilege for US foreigners needing health care when far from home. In Luke's story the other nine, presumably Jews, may have been less appreciative since they were healed by one of their own, Jesus, seen as one of their Rabbis, a teacher roaming Galilee. But the Samaritan, knowing that he was not well-liked in those parts, was caught off guard by this Healer's care for him too. He just had to come back and say thank you because, having been healed of leprosy, his life would never be the same. And it was all because of Jesus.

We ask our children to follow the example of the one who says thank you. But are we more likely, as adults, to follow the example of the other nine? Perhaps they did not return to say thanks because the healing was an expected gift. I mean Jesus was out there healing everyone in sight, wasn't He? If they chose to view their gift of healing in this fashion, they were missing out on something much larger. They may have been making a mistake many of us make daily in overlooking the value of a gift simply because it's one gift given to many.

Let's consider the response of a receiver when the gift he receives is one given indiscriminately. The sun rises on all of us. The water that refreshes us is in the water cooler for anyone to use. That philanthropist gave a gift for the whole town. The school principal is just doing his job when he greets every student coming into the school. There's no reason to give thanks for these pleasures because they're meant for all.

And yet, with the act of recognizing the pleasure, the receiver's enjoyment is multiplied. In other words, if the receiver misses the fact that a gift has been given, he overlooks the joy of the gift. The community park is there for all to see, but only enjoyed by those who notice the flowers or cool, shaded park benches. The one who makes time to delight in the park can find an even deeper joy in recognizing the benefactor's generosity. And the park patron will be uplifted if that thanks is somehow expressed. Thus, the joy of a gift given can be multiplied threefold by expressing thanks. First, there is the joy of the gift. Second, there is joy in recognition. Third, there is joy for the giver when thanks is spoken.

A foreigner was healed, and maybe surprised by the gift of healing. He alone—as the one not expecting a gift—says thanks. What unexpected gifts are awaiting us today? Who can we surprise with our expressions of thanks?

IMPENDING DESTRUCTION

Then Jesus asks, "Were not ten made clean? But the other nine, where are they? Were none of them found to return and give praise to God except this foreigner? ... Get up and go on your way; your faith has made you well."
Luke 17:11–19

There is more to consider in this story of unrestrained thanks given by the Samaritan to his healer, Jesus. Only he came back to thank Jesus, prostrating himself at Jesus' feet. I must say, I have never expressed my thanks in such a demonstrative way. Jesus' response is a significant part of the story and gives us a good reason to continue to think about this Samaritan's thanks.

After he is healed, the Samaritan comes back to Jesus to express his thanks and only then does Jesus pronounce the Samaritan well: "Your faith has made you well." Did Jesus mean that it wasn't the healing that made him well, but the his response to the healing? This scripture lesson may be trying to tell us that it's in the recognition of and thanks for gifts from God that we can be made well.

The NRSV Bible notes explain that the Greek used in this passage could also be translated as "your faith has rescued you from impending destruction." The Samaritan has been rescued from what impending destruction? Before Jesus made this pronouncement, the Samaritan had already been cured of the leprosy. What other destruction was there?

Is there destruction in not saying thank you? What comes of our daily living if we don't recognize cause for thankful living? Overlooking all there is to be thankful for leads to a life void of joy or full of self —that sounds like "impending destruction" to me! Disregarding the service of others, which makes our days better, contributes to our own daily demise. Failure to notice God's constant gifts to us personally can make us negative, mean-spirited folks. Maybe I am painting with too broad a brush here, so let me say this: *for me*, failure to notice gifts God has given to me every day, makes me a more negative, unpleasant person.

As I have said, I run most mornings and often pray while I'm running. A big part of that ritual is so that I can keep my thankful self in check. While starting my day, I look for new reasons to be glad for another day and thank God in prayer. In a way, I am trying to avoid that impending destruction that Jesus speaks of in this verse. I want to keep myself from focusing on the hurts of the day: the physical pain of aging or the emotional pain of being in relationships. Attention to thanks leads to a life of impending devotion instead of destruction.

Luke's story of one man's thanks is a lesson for our young children, yes, but one that we as adults must revisit to hear its more challenging warning. We could be facing impending destruction or we could be made well.

PART 3
LIVE IT!

LIVE IT!

When dieting, some look at everything in terms of caloric intake. When short on cash, daily activity is defined by how much it will cost. When bored or busy, every minute is counted, whether it's dragging on or flying by. My point is this: we can view the passing of our days from an endless number of vantage points. I am advocating that we all consider viewing life from a perspective of thankfulness and living each day as an expression of that mindset. Saying thanks is just the tip of the iceberg. We'll seek more substantial ways of expressing gratitude.

Grateful for life's blessings, we'll want to share what we've received. Thankfulness will spill in and out of our wallets, our agendas, and our hearts. An attitude of utter appreciativeness will pull our attentions toward the needs of others, even those completely unrelated to our present state of thankfulness. In other words, we'll be living our thanks with those who never gave us reason to say thanks.

And what will living thanks look like? Thankful living compels us to sing, to shout, to advocate, to empower, to forgive, to overcome. As demonstrated by Jesus, thankful living blesses others with the assurance of God's presence. With an attitude of gratitude for wealth, health, nature, relationships, and blessings we may dance with delight or labor with love. Thankful living simply makes the world a better place to be in.

11

HIS EXAMPLE

Jesus gave us examples of living thanks in His own words and deeds. We see His example alive today in those who are lamplighters, living prayers, and "Life is good" advocates.

LAMPLIGHTERS

"…let your light shine before others…" Matthew 5:14–16

Some might say today is a gloomy day. It may be a Monday—back to school, or back to work and for some, and that's not a cause for joy. It may be a rainy day after a weekend of sunshine and blue skies—it can be tough to get going in a dreary mist. It may be a late autumn day when daylight continues to dwindle and we walk out in the morning dark—ugh. We know that winter can't be far off.

Wait just a minute here! Where are we going with all this? Where's the joy of gratitude? Where's the hope of thankfulness? Where's the light of optimism? This sounds too dark.

The story goes that in his childhood, from his sick bed, Robert Louis Stevenson looked out into the dark streets and watched the lamplighter at work. He said the man could knock holes in the darkness. Every time he climbed the ladder to kindle the streetlights of Edinburgh, Scotland, he knocked out some of the gloom of the night, and perhaps some of the despair of a sickly, young boy.

Being one who can see and express his thanks is one with the power to knock holes in the darkness. Reflecting back even a thin beam of light makes him a nemesis of the dark. A thankful outlook will say of a rainy Monday morning, "I'm so thankful that the rain held off so we could enjoy the weekend. It's a blessing to have a job to return to on Mondays. No sun glare to contend with on this morning's drive!"

Let us use this ancient vocational title as a modern day title given to those who make it their ambition to knock holes in the dark gloom and despair that can overwhelm. For Reverend Samuel Billy Kyles, Dr. Martin Luther King, Jr. was a lamplighter and he knocked holes in the darkness of Memphis (read more at NPR on the page for 17 January 2010, and find a great interview by Liane Hansen). My neighbor, Darlene, is a lamplighter in my world. She told me one gloomy morning how beautifully the day was starting out. Another is a friend who posted a video of her three toddlers dancing with glee. She could just as easily told us how tired she is trying to parent her little ones and not a one of us would begrudge her telling that truth. Instead, she chose to be thankful and light a light. Amy, a missionary awarded sabbatical time, returned to Sarajevo because in that place she sees people full of lamp lighting power, and because she too has looked for and found light in places where others only see shadows.

Do you know a lamplighter? Have you seen the need for a lamplighter? Could you light a lamp and knock a hole the darkness somewhere today? Jesus says we would never light a lamp and then hide it under a bushel. Isn't it also true that we would never want to see something thank-worthy and then keep it quietly to ourselves or simply forget all about it? Let the thanks in our lives propel us into action, lighting fires, warming hearts, illuminating the truth, reflecting the glow, and being light unto the world. Is that too much to ask on a gloomy Monday?

A LIVING PRAYER

"Then He took the cup, and after giving thanks He gave it to them, saying, 'Drink from it, all of you; for this is my blood of the covenant, which is poured out for many for the forgiveness of sins.'" Matthew 26:26–28

When Jesus shared the Last Supper with His disciples, and ultimately with all of us, He became a living prayer. Imagine prayer as our awareness of the presence of God. And then consider that Jesus gave us this sacrament as a ritual reminder of His gift of God's presence, given to us for all time. Jesus became a living, dying, risen prayer for us.

"The way is dark, the road is steep. But, He's become my eyes to see, the strength to climb, my grief to bear; the Savior lives inside me there… In these trials of life I find another voice inside my mind. He comforts me and bids me live inside the love the Father gives… In your love I find release, a haven from my unbelief. Take my life and let me be a living prayer, my God, to Thee."

Alison Krauss shares her reflections in this song, "A Living Prayer." From a place of darkness, doubt, grief, and trials, Alison finds shelter in God's presence and a desire to live as a prayer, a blessing, for others. In other words, it's not from her strength that she wishes to serve, but rather, from her weakness. Also from His weakness—His ultimate weakness of giving up His life on the cross—Jesus becomes the strongest force in history, a prayer for all of humanity.

Now what does any of this have to do with thankfulness? Here is the connection I see: We will all, eventually, find ourselves in a place of significant weakness. It may be moral weakness, financial weakness, physical weakness, or illness. Our confusion, lack of skills, or insufficient direction could be our weakness. And from that position, certain of our inability to do enough of something of value, we want to give up. Instead, if we can find something to give thanks for, that can be our lifeline out of despair. That can be what pulls us out of self-pity and into awareness of our potential. From a place of thankfulness, we can be a living prayer. In her song, Alison found God's comfort as her thankful thread. For Jesus, it may have been the same—as well as a love for God's people—that gave Him the thankful thread to pull Him through the last hours of His life among us.

It may be our thanks for a small piece of who we still are. It may be thanks for those who surround us, who we love so deeply. Maybe it's the gratitude we feel for the earth's magnificent beauty and wonder. We may feel thanks for a dream or a hope we harbor within ourselves. It may be the unwavering belief that we are fully loved by our Creator. Any one of these causes for thanks can become our inspiration. And from this "attitude of gratitude" we find the courage to move forward. Our determination transforms us into a living prayer.

Sam is a woman of inconceivable courage. For me, she is a living prayer. Stricken by two strokes in the spring of her senior year of high school, it seemed all her future hopes were crushed. She had been a top athlete, an amazing scholar, and a school leader. The strokes appeared to strip all of that from her. Yet, through her struggle to recover, she has become a living prayer for so many in our community. I asked her what has given her the courage to move forward through rehab and reconstruct her life. Sam replied: "There is no other way; I either get better or live my life in a wheelchair… I want to be me again." She holds on to a prayer that she can continue to recover. And lest we think Sam defines herself solely as an athlete, as one bound by her physical abilities, she goes on to explain: "Honestly though, it showed me that sports aren't everything. In high school, everyone thinks that's what life's about, which is okay, but really it's not." From her reply, I read that Sam has always had an internal sense of gratitude for who she was. That attitude of gratitude is a part of what strengthens her to appreciate who she is now, and who she is working hard to become. For Sam, maybe thankfulness is a part of what gives her the power to be a living prayer for the rest of us.

If I can find the courage to pray, as Alison sung, maybe I can become a living prayer. I long to be an example for others of God's presence in this world.

LIFE IS GOOD!

"Let the little children come to me; do not stop them'… and He took them up into His arms, laid His hands on them, and blessed them." Mark 10:13–16

Life is good! Kathy reminded the congregation of this during worship one morning, pointing to the logo on her t-shirt from the Life is Good® product line. She spoke the words common in my heart too, about all the good that is in her life, our lives: loving family, happy childhood memories, enough of everything. Her tone changed as she read statistics concerning children whose lives are lacking the basic good and necessary elements of safety, health, and love.

Again and again, I am reminded of the power of thanks. Kathy started with recognition of numerous reasons for thanks, of all that makes her life good. She called us to do the same, even if she never actually used the words "thank you." Think of those things that inflate our hearts with thanks. And then with a big heart, go out and care for those whose lives lack the necessary elements of thankful living.

This got me thinking about the Life is Good® (LIG) line of products, and sent me researching online. Imagine my surprise in finding that LIG's success has brought them to a place where they are able to support outreach efforts. "Optimism can take you anywhere" is their logo, and for this company, optimistic products and management have taken them into the lives of children in trauma, providing a safe place for healing experiences through play. How does one transform a t-shirt shop into a foundation for children in need?

This is thankful living at work. As I write, think, pray, and preach the message of thankful living, this is the outcome I hope to inspire. When our faith calls us to say thank you, our lives respond with action like this of the LIG Foundation. When we find ourselves in a place like Kathy, where we acknowledge we are living a very, very good life, we can be propelled beyond words of gratitude and into a life of giving.

The Gospel of Mark tells us that Jesus took children in His arms and blessed them. He reminded the adults gathered there to never prevent children from being with Jesus. If we agree that life is good, then let's put our good life to work making life good for children and everyone else. May we enable today's children to feel the loving touch of Jesus through our own loving actions—inspired by our thankful state.

12

NO HOLDING BACK

When I receive a special box of dark chocolate, I'm careful not to over-indulge. I want to make it last. There is a time for restraint. Likewise, I use my favorite perfume sparingly; there is a time for conservation. However, there is also a time for—a need for—an outright explosion of grateful expression! Sometimes it is best to hold nothing back, to use it all, to have no leftovers! Living thanks can mean giving it all up now because we have faith that there is more thankworthy living yet to come.

NO LEFTOVERS

"And the flesh of your thanksgiving sacrifice of well-being shall be eaten on the day it is offered; you shall not leave any of it until morning." Leviticus 7:11–15

Throughout their childhood, we have encouraged our children to write thank-you notes for gifts received for Christmas and their birthdays. Other parents in our family likewise encouraged a written thank you by not allowing their child to play with her gifts until after those notes were written and mailed. For some, that ritual of a written note is being transformed into thanks by means of texts, tweets, or facebook wall messages left for the gift givers. Sometimes a simple verbal thank you is spoken at the time the gift is received or opened. Maybe our efforts of thankful expression are being boiled down to what is simplest and quickest.

In the Book of Leviticus, entire chapters are devoted to ways people can offer their thanks to God, as well as their grief and regret. Scripture records ritualistic ways of asking for forgiveness or expressing gratitude. This is done through a series of ritual offerings and sacrifices. As Christians, we have come to see Jesus' death on the cross as replacing our need to offer ritual sacrifice for our sins, but certainly we must continue to offer thanks. Leviticus 7:11–15 describes ways of offering a thanksgiving sacrifice that seem nothing short of foreign and odd—at least at first glance.

All of the offerings are "given" to God, as an expression of thanks. What that looks like is explained in these verses: A portion of everything offered goes to the priest; he gets to eat it. The rest is to be eaten that day by the worshiper and his guests. The worshiper who brings the offering must be ready to celebrate in a big way. *The Interpreter's One-Volume Commentary On The Bible* goes on the say that in the case of this type of offering, the worshiper had better be sure his guest list is large enough to consume everything brought to God that day. It's like a Thanksgiving dinner with no leftovers allowed. Everything is thankfully, joyfully shared and feasted upon that day.

To me Leviticus is saying, if you're going to give thanks, go big or go home! A tweet post of less than 140 characters isn't going to cut it. Saying "thanks" with a weak half smile isn't what the Levites had in mind either. And when you want to tell God thank you, be sure everyone you know hears about it and gets to be a part of your thanks ritual.

This is not to say there's no room for private moments of thankful expression. Our silent prayers of thanks to God are a vital part of our daily relationship with Him. Likewise, I am still very glad for all the thank-you notes I find in my mailbox after Christmas, showers, and birthdays. There is nothing wrong with writing as an expression of gratitude to friends and family. And I will continue daily to say thanks to the countless folks who brighten my day with their courtesies and kindness.

But, there needs to be a place in our lives for big, all-out, grand thank yous to God. For example: Thanksgiving day, Christmas day, worship that brings us to our feet in praise, weddings, birthdays, celebrations of special people and special events, inaugurations, and many others.

What makes these events **big**? Let's not assume that making something expensive will guarantee that it's meaningful or praiseworthy. Looking back at Leviticus, we can see that a big event comes from one's voluntary act of devotion, not his/her compulsion to act in an expected way. That's right. All the sacrificial offerings described in these chapters are the result of one's call of conscience, not a requirement of one's faith community. A celebration initiated by love and thanks to God, and a desire to pronounce those sentiments to the world is a great place to start.

When Dave and his partner had completed five years in business together, there was overwhelming joy in my heart. I knew that what we had come through to get to that point was due to their hard work and God's good care. And so we had a big surprise party for them. The food was simple. The guests were friends and supporters. The mood was festive. It was my way to say to the world, "I thank God for my husband and his determination!"

Last year, when my sister-in-law and brother found themselves in Ohio just days before Christmas for her father's funeral, we mourned their loss. However, a few short days later, we celebrated Christmas with extra joy because they were there with us, rather than far away in California.

When our daughter received more than seven awards for her seventh grade academic achievements, we spread the word with enthusiasm. We thanked God for her in a variety of ways, being sure to call out-of-town family, post the awards on the dining room wall, and hug her ceaselessly.

You know that you do it too. You find yourself at times overwhelmed with joy and thanks from life's events. Perhaps the lesson from Leviticus is twofold. First, simply be sure to let God in on those times. Remember to invite God to the surprise parties. Be sure God is seated with you at holiday meals. Remember to call God and share all the details of the magnificent win you're celebrating. Second, let others in on your God-directed thanks. Let people know that you are thankful to God for where you are in life. Like a big party or a festive meal, be sure to feed as many as you can with your joy and thankfulness. Share it all! And don't throw away the leftovers. Keep sharing the thanksgiving meal with everyone you know until every last morsel of thanks has been consumed.

EXTRAVAGANT THANKS!

"Mary took a pound of costly perfume made of pure nard, anointed Jesus' feet, and wiped them with her hair." John 12:1–8 (and maybe on to Deuteronomy 15:10,11)

Herein lies a story of "extravagant thanks!" Such are the words of Reverend Chad Delaney one Sunday during worship as he shared his thoughts concerning the story of Mary anointing the feet of Jesus. Pouring the expensive perfume on the feet of the one who raised her brother from the dead, Mary wiped Jesus' feet with her hair. Did she realize that Jesus' return to Bethany was dangerous because of all those who sought to kill him? Did she realize that in using a perfume most frequently used to prepare a body for burial that her acts were a foretelling of Jesus' own death? Could Mary have foreseen the argument that would result about the plight of the poor and this extravagant waste? Did she know that in her home that day was the one who would betray her Lord, and her act presented Jesus with an opportunity to confront the betrayer?

In those moments, Mary's thoughts were centered on one person. Her thoughts were with Jesus and her love for him. She was, I believe, consumed with gratitude for all that He had done for her, saving her brother, giving her a new understanding of life, and presenting her with an opportunity for a deep relationship with her Creator. "He has restored my dignity and saved my flesh and blood," these are the words Chad used to express Mary's center of focus that day with Jesus in her home.

In Jesus' previous visit to Bethany, Mary's brother was wrapped in the cloths of burial, enclosed in a tomb for four days when Jesus called to him from the tomb and restored Lazarus' life. One can only imagine the chaos that ensued. Many mourners were there with Mary and her sister, Martha. Some must have run to unbind Lazarus; others hugged the sisters. Some may have run off in fear or with enthusiasm to gossip—a good story on their lips. The gathered crowd included some trying to explain away the miracle and others remarking on Jesus' tears. A group of conspirators compared stories as they prepared a statement for the Pharisees. Mary, Martha, and Lazarus most likely found themselves reunited in a family embrace, drenched in their own tears of joy. Knowing her, Martha was the one most likely to have insisted they return home and clean Lazarus up, so they headed home.

On the day of Lazarus' healing, Mary's last recorded words for Jesus had the sting of anger and disappointment in them for she spoke before the miracle: "Lord, if you had been here, my brother would not have died" (John 11:32). All the chaos that followed would understandably distract Mary from sharing her words of apology for Jesus and thanks for His miracle. In the Gospel's next chapter she is reunited with her Lord and brother's savior. In their home, as their guest, the family expresses their thanks in three distinct ways. Martha has busied herself with preparing and serving dinner to the guest of honor. Lazarus seats himself at the table with Jesus, presenting Him with all the attention that was previously directed at Lazarus himself. And Mary does the unthinkable, spilling perfume on the guest's feet, ointment costing a year's wages. She uses it all rather than parceling out a few drops. For finally, Mary can express her unbridled thanks for her Lord, for our Jesus.

There are times when giving thanks requires giving one's all. There can be no holding back. Words alone cannot fully express the deep gratitude. Neither money nor gifts can fully cover one's indebtedness. One's thankfulness sometimes requires a personally unique effort demanding the best of that one's spirit. Stop and think about your own life. When has such thanks been appropriate and were you courageous enough to give it?

For me as a child, there was some sort of disconnect between the words on a page and the firing neurons in my head. Few people in my life recognized the reading trouble I was having or had faith in my potential. Mr. Bowdich, my fourth grade teacher, was one. My mom was another. Mr. Bowdich recommended that I have several reading tests done to see if I was dyslexic. When the tests showed no such problem, he devised personal reading incentives for me. Being singled out as one who received special attention from my teacher was incentive enough and my reading efforts doubled. His efforts were a start and my mother's work complimented Mr. Bowdich's plan. This was a great start, but the work continued long after that teacher's time with me.

Throughout my grade school years, my mom sat with me as she read, and then I read my classroom textbooks, my homework assignments, my papers, projects, reports, and library books. Sometimes she would read a page, then I would read a page. On really bad days, she'd read a page and I'd try to read a paragraph, stumbling over words like "an" or "of." As I moved into to high school, I read on my own, but she read and corrected my writing assignments, placing a lightly marked check at the start of any sentence with an error. I had to find the mistakes and correct them myself, teaching me to proofread my own writing.

I vividly remember babysitting our neighbor boys who could read their storybooks aloud better than I could. Although my reading skills had improved, now my brain didn't seem to have a clear-cut path between what my eyes saw and what my lips could say. Years before I became a mother, I fretted the time when I would want to read aloud to my children. Furthermore, I wondered how I would find the time and drive to read with my children for hours on end as my mother did with me. What if my children had reading disabilities like me? Would I be able to help them? Nearly 20 years before I even became a mother, I already wondered if I would be able to read with them.

As a 28-year-old adult I came to a city church in Cleveland, and as staff, I had weekly responsibilities that included reading aloud during the worship service. My love of God drove my labors of love, giving me the courage to stand before a portion of God's people in Cleveland and do what I thought I would never be able to do even in the privacy of my own home with young children. I learned to read aloud in front of people, and even came to relish the opportunity to serve God this way. For me this was an all out expression of gratitude to God for Mr. Bowdich and my mom. But, it didn't stop there.

Nearly six years later, I began reading to my son and soon thereafter, to my daughter. We made time every night and almost every afternoon to read lots of books. We brought home stacks of library books: baby books, picture books, storybooks, fantasy, and adventure books. We began reading chapter books together, 200–300 pages long. Both children read above their grade-level throughout grade school. Hundreds of hours—probably thousands of hours—were spent just sitting on the couch together, reading.

There were days and nights when I was tired and there was work to be done. My nighttime walking group of friends wanted my company. Volunteer work called for me. Sometimes sleep beckoned to each of us. But my children and I read together. And I thanked my mom and Mr. Bowdich with more than words. I poured out my love for them, and for my children, with my own expression of extravagant thanks! Like Mary offering up a bottle of expensive perfume, I held the sands of an hourglass. Together, with my church and my children over the years, we poured the sand out. We gave it our all! And I expressed my thanks in a manner similar to that which Chad expressed in his sermon, "not with a few drops, but open it up and let it all pour out!"

RECKLESS ABANDON

"Let us come into His presence with thanksgiving; let us make a joyful noise to Him with songs of praise." Psalms 95:2

We have two children who play basketball on different school teams, and we all enjoy watching occasional college or NBA games on TV, too. Sometimes we even attend school games for the other teams, and so there are weeks when we'll attend six games and watch several others on TV. Yes, I know it's kind of sick. There are days when I come home with a sore throat, barely able to talk from all the cheering. Still, the next day I'm there in the stands shouting for my kid and their teammates again. Okay, I'll be totally honest: I waste some of that shouting on the refs (they may all be nice guys but sometimes I wonder if they're wearing blinders on the court).

The energy that the fans expel for ten players running up and down a court with an orange ball is not seen as anything unusual or inappropriate. This kind of reaction to a sporting event takes place every day in our society. But if we take it out of context, analyze it, and try to make sense of it, we all come out looking a little unstable. During my week of significant activity, there is no time that I express my emotions more vehemently, more stridently, more deeply than I do while in the gym.

I watch the news and see children in Haiti alone, homeless, and starving, but don't scream at that injustice. I read about the new science advancements for green energy and don't stand and cheer in joy. I worship with my church family and actually hear the words that our early Christian brothers and sisters heard in their worship and don't sing out the glory of that privilege.

Psalm 95, like many others, calls us to sing to the Lord—**make a joyful noise!**

I'm good at making joyful noises when Amy gets another rebound, or Andy makes a good pass, or our team gets that orange ball into the basket. What about using that energy and intensity to thank God and praise God? Our churches aren't really the kind of place where a yelling crowd is often heard—even yelling words of praise. In fact, I've never heard the folks in my churches yell, except at a ball game we happened to be attending together. And although we'll occasionally sing out a beloved hymn with loud voices, usually our singing sounds more like a response to a requirement than a reaction of sheer joy and praise.

At this time, I don't have a good explanation for this imbalance, where we cheer with unabashed enthusiasm at a sporting event, a rock concert, or a political rally, but use such restraint in expressing our love for God. But, maybe it's something the Psalmist recognized too, and why the author saw the need to call the faithful to make joyful noise and come into God's presence with thanksgiving. When as deeply immersed in God's presence and blessings as we are, do we become desensitized to God's love, forgetting how awesome it all is?

The Psalmist wrote then and we read now that we need to reexamine our blessed surroundings and allow ourselves to fully sing out, yell, and even cheer for God! Our gratitude calls for a response of "reckless abandon!" Those are the words of Dr. Ken Chalker, pastor of an amazing congregation in Cleveland, Ohio. He frequently reminds his parishioners to go into the world with God's love, sharing it with reckless abandon! In other words, live our love and shout our thanks with all the enthusiasm shared on the game-winning court.

WEARING OUR THANKS UNDER OUR NOSES

"And be thankful… and with gratitude in your hearts sing… And whatever you do, in word or deed, do everything in the name of the Lord Jesus, giving thanks to God through Him." Colossians 3:12–17

Sit and smile.

These were the simple instructions given to the author Elizabeth Gilbert while under the tutelage of an Indonesian medicine man. Her story comes from the book *Eat, Pray, Love*. The timing for her was especially intriguing, since she had just spent four months learning about meditation in India. But her new instructor used these simple instructions to guide her meditation efforts in Bali.

I have also been following the simple instructions of the ancient medicine man, in my own hyper-active way. I don't sit well. I don't stay still well. And so in my daily activity, I have been trying to just smile. It sounds embarrassingly simple. Just move the muscles in my face to consciously smile.

It's after I put the smile on my face that my thought patterns begin to transform. Pleasant thoughts begin to pry open the shuttered doors in my brain. I realize that a breeze is cooling my sun-baked cheek. Or I recall my daughter's kind words from earlier in the day. I notice that the morning headache is gone and I start looking forward to seeing my husband for lunch. The smile that I had to methodically place on my face is no longer a struggle to maintain. Instead, it's as if my heart has taken over and my face is responding with a face-splitting smile. Sometimes I even feel myself suppressing a little giggle.

Recording this on paper seems so absurd, even silly. But, the medicine man's advice is medicine to my spirit. And I could sing, "I've got the joy, joy, joy, joy down in my heart!"

At other times, maintaining a smile demands more attention and work on my part. There may be a deep anger in my heart holding me back, someone I should just forgive and get over it. It's hard to smile when I have hatred brewing within. But even if I'm in the midst of an internal pity party, the forced smile seems to be the right prescription.

The verses from Colossians chapter 3 are Paul's "sit and smile" lecture. In just these six verses Paul says, "be thankful…with gratitude…giving thanks." Paul reminds us to be forgiving, and then to be thankful. Paul tells us to share the word of Jesus, and then to be full of gratitude. Paul tells us to be ruled by Jesus' peace, and then to give thanks!

Gratitude brings a smile to one's face. Start counting your blessings and feel the corners of your mouth lift upward. Or, try to imagine a Thanksgiving dinner table where the guests look glum and sour-faced. It just doesn't work. When we are thinking thoughts of gratitude we are gratefully smiling! Try it next time you're stuck in traffic. Let thankfulness flood your conscience. A smile will begin to light up your face. Then, all the drivers stuck in cars around you will begin to stare and wonder what you're up to. Just keep smiling.

So what is it with a smile? Why is it so crucial to wear our thankfulness on our sleeves? No. Actually, we wear it under our noses, in a smile. Maybe it's just a nice gift to share with all those we see. And maybe it's a nice gift we can give ourselves. And maybe it's a nice gift we can share with our Creator, a way of saying thanks. Sit and smile. And live your thanks.

13
PAY IT FORWARD

In the 1955 novel by Robert Heinlein, Between Planets, a character is given help in a very desperate time. He tells his benefactor, "… I'll pay it back first chance." Surprisingly, the character is instructed, "Instead, pay it forward to some other brother who needs it." The concept is similar to that shared by Catherine Hyde in her book, Pay It Forward, and the subsequent movie. When our gratitude is embodied in kindness toward another, this is living our thanks. And to do so can be costly, life altering, and a heavenly encounter.

LIVE THANKS, TOUCH HEAVEN

"To speak gratitude is courteous and pleasant, to enact gratitude is generous and noble, but to live gratitude is to touch heaven." Johannes A. Gaertner

To voice one's thanks is a kind gesture, but just saying thanks isn't always enough. Doing thanks, not just saying it, takes more effort. How do we do thanks? Expressing gratitude by action is doing thanks. Action that recognizes the effort of the one deserving thanks is appropriate. Here are a few examples: "Thanks for a great dinner. You must have really worked hard on that. Let me clear the table for you." "Teacher, thank you for loaning me your pencil" might be followed by returning the pencil and bringing a pencil to class next time. "Thanks for the ride" feels more sincere when the rider was ready to be picked up at the designated time. "Thank you for being so patient" is said, and then patience is likewise shared.

In fact, doing thanks can be expanded to living thanks. Not only do we say and do thanks for the individual who was kind to us, but we also act in a way that elicits the thanks of others. In other words, living thanks is not just being nice to the one who has been nice to you; it's looking for opportunities to offer niceties to the unsuspecting. Make a meal or a snack for your family without being asked. Loan a pencil, paper, or book to a classmate. Help another get where he needs to be by car, escort, or other arrangements. Be patient with others, especially those who find it difficult to share patience.

There will be times when saying thanks to the deserving person is not possible. Maybe we forgot to say thanks when we could. Perhaps we didn't recognize the need to say thanks until much later. Maybe we didn't know who to thank or the one we wanted to thank is no longer available. In these cases, creative, thankful expression is needed and living thanks is the way to go. We now try to offer the good that was done for us to others.

As I discussed earlier, in grade school, I had severe difficulty concentrating on reading. Much of my classwork went undone because I wasn't able to focus on assignments and understand the reading I had to do. Stacks of unfinished papers accumulated inside my desk, hidden behind my pencil box. Hiding the unfinished work was affecting my self-image and confidence. Finally, Mr. Bowdich, my fourth grade teacher, previously mentioned in this book, found unique ways to motivate me. He told me I was smart, helped me set goals, celebrated small accomplishments, and just said hello and asked how I was doing each day. In doing so, he directed me down a new academic path. Fourth grade was a turning point for me.

I sent Mr. Bowdich a college graduation announcement some 12 years later, but didn't receive a reply. Having lost contact with my elementary school teacher, and yet still wanting to say thanks, meant I would have to find a less conventional way to do it. Now as a substitute teacher, I look for the opportunity to live my thanks to Mr. Bowdich by encouraging troubled student. Patiently, in the one day I have with her, I find some sincere cause for praise for a disheartened student. Or I'll stand with a boy, encouraging him to concentrate as he works through his math problem, congratulating him with the words, "I knew you could do it; try the next one." Small gestures of confidence in these students are like words written on the thank-you note I never actually wrote to Mr. Bowdich. I symbolically write each word hoping that it may motivate students to work a little harder and think a little better of themselves.

The idea of sharing with others what was first shared with you is living your thanks. It's more than saying thanks to the giver. It's more than doing thanks for the giver. It's reflecting the generous behavior of the giver upon others. It's giving, not because we might ourselves receive thanks or gifts as a result of our giving. It's giving motivated by gratitude for receiving from another what we needed, wanted, or enjoyed. Therefore, we expect nothing more from our gift. If our thankful expression motivates others to live their thanks, it's a bonus. And the kind works of one person may benefit another and another and another. Living thanks can initiate an endless avalanche of good.

If you hold the door for me I can say, "thank you" and the exchange is through. Or I could hold the next door for you, and again the exchange is finished. Or I could say thanks and then hold the door for another, who may see it fit to hold the door for another, who may hold another door for another person, who could… I hope you get the point. And if the initial act of kindness was larger, the results could be much, much bigger. If you help me rebuild my home after a flood and I, with thanks to you many years later, contribute my funds and talents to Habitat for Humanity, that gift could affect several more families. Those families may contribute their time and effort to their local neighborhood rehab, which could propel a whole neighborhood of families into better futures.

Like Johannes Gaertner, I like to hear someone say thank you to me. It's nice to be appreciated. Words are pleasant to hear. But I know that my actions have had a genuine impact when, because of my good works, someone repays another with more good. Is it possible that cascading acts of kindness bring us all closer to experiencing heaven on earth? So, tell me thanks, show me thanks, but better yet, live your thanks.

A COSTLY THANK YOU

"Then Mary said, 'Here am I, a servant of the Lord; let it be with me according to your word.' Then the angel departed from her." Luke 1:26–56

Sometimes we do not say our thanks. Sometimes we just live the words.

Mary never said thank you for the honor of being chosen as the mother of our Creator's Son. In these verses, the start of her journey, she may not have fully grasped her thankfulness. She may not have even felt thankful in those moments. Scared, alone, frightened, in trouble, these come to mind as feelings that may have flooded her conscience as the angel spoke to her and then departed.

When given an unreal amount of responsibility, thankfulness is not always the first thing that comes to mind. Making use of our gifts and talents can be a huge responsibility, and sometimes the thought of living up to our potential doesn't lead us into an attitude of gratitude. Mary sets before us an inspirational example as a woman given an epic role of responsibility and living up to her call. The angel announced that she would be a mother, that she would do so at a young age without a husband yet, and that the child would be our Savior.

As I understand it, during this period of history young Jewish women would pray for the privilege of bearing the child who would become the King, the Messiah, as foretold by the prophets. I doubt that any of those women dreamed that they would be called to do so as an unwed girl in the poor social standing that Mary found herself in. Understandably, Mary may not have seen herself fit to raise the King, nor would those around her.

If, in fact, Mary did feel unworthy, unfit, or unprepared to become the mother of Jesus, she still accepted the angel's task, for she was willing to be God's servant. Luke tells us that Mary then traveled to be with her cousin, Elizabeth, who immediately recognized Mary's unborn child as our Lord. Mary responded to her cousin's reception with a beautiful song of praise and blessing for God (verses 46–55). Although the word "thanks" is absent, Mary's thankfulness permeates the Magnificat, as these verses have come to be known.

As I said at the start, even if words of thanks were not recorded, Mary's life read as one thankful for God's intervention. Scripture records that Mary treasured the experiences in her heart (Luke 2:19, 51). Various Gospel verses record Mary's continued presence in her son's life, although with little detail. Mary raised a son who knew the Hebrew traditions, loved Yahweh, prayed constantly, and was kind and loving. She was aware from the start that her son, as well as herself, would suffer (Luke 2:33–35) and she still committed herself to being God's servant and Jesus' mother.

Every Christmas there are numerous gifts we receive wrapped in paper and bows that we sit and write thank-you notes for. There are also parties, favors, and holiday outings that fill us with gratitude, and we say our thanks for those too. What about the other gifts that we face that time of year, and actually, throughout our lives? What of the gift of responsibility? What of the call to hard work? What of the discovery of talents that we could employ for the betterment of others? These are gifts that we can only live our thanks for. If we accept the charge and live to our potential, we write words of thanks on walls that build a better world.

Our daughter received a slushy maker for her birthday last year. She uses it almost every day. The device crushes ice cubes into snowy, fine crystals that she douses with flavored syrup. Any evening she craves the frozen treat, she'll offer to make one for the rest of us too. She fills coffee mugs with snow and syrup and delivers them to us as we watch TV or finish homework. Then, she cleans up after herself (usually) and makes more ice cubes for another day. Within a few short weeks all her flavoring bottles were nearly empty. She went online to survey her options and discovered there is a high market price for slushy syrup. At that point, she began to question the way she chose to use her gift. It was costing her time (making all those extra snacks for others) as well as a ton of money for supplies! Meanwhile, the rest of us were the beneficiaries of Amy's birthday present. She has since ordered more syrup (for which she received unsolicited donations) and she continues to make slushies for us. She even brought the machine along with her for a family gathering and made refreshments for all her aunts, uncles, and cousins. Amy has accepted her call to frozen treat supplier. She is very grateful for that birthday gift.

Amy received a gift and now gives to us, with some cost to herself.

God gave Mary a gift that required her to give in return.

I know the comparison is ridiculous, but therein lies a lesson. Choosing to use our gifts and abilities for the benefit of others is an expression of thankful living. Saying thanks isn't as vital as living thanks with our whole being. And sometimes living our thanks comes at a personal cost.

Here I am, said Mary, willing to be a servant, willing to live in accordance with the word of God for my life. Wow.

THANKS IS GOOD MEDICINE

*"Each of you must give as you have made up your minds, not reluctantly
or under compulsion, for God loves a cheerful giver... You will be enriched
in every way for your generosity, which will produce thanksgiving to God
through us." II Corinthians 9:7–12*

Gratitude is good medicine. Seriously. Gratitude initiates the body's creation
of oxytocin, a hormone clinically shown to enhance trust, empathy, and generosity. Oxytocin also decreases one's sense of fear and stress. In other words,
being thankful increases one's overall sense of well-being. Paul reminds us that
God loves a cheerful **giver**. Modern science tells us that giving creates a cheerful **receiver**. Apparently, this was not news to Paul, who wrote long ago about
the benefits of sharing for the receiver who, of course, is blessed by needs being
met. The receiver is also filled with joy in recognizing God's presence in her
life. Furthermore, she may be transformed into a giver herself.

Sharing, Paul tells us, "supplies the needs" and one is blessed. Whether it's
shelter, food, clothing, or a kind word, what is shared with us and meets our
needs, blesses us. Regardless of the specific need, knowing someone is aware
of our need and chooses to help is an affirmation of our worth in their sight.

Sharing, Paul goes on to say, "overflows with many thanksgivings to
God." As one's needs are met, she comes to acknowledge God's activity in her
life and joy abounds. Although God has always been in her midst, a growling
stomach can drown out the music sent by God in the songbirds, and a war-
torn world can make one blind to a night sky of God's stars. When blessed with
what one needs, it seems that she can acknowledge the flood of God's blessings
and she is saturated with joy.

Sharing has transformative power. When blessed by another's generosity,
the recipient is inspired to seek opportunities to spread his joy and share when
he is able. One example is found in Nacilien Josue, a 10-year-old from Haiti
who benefited from a unique ministry of One Great Hour of Sharing after
the 2010 earthquake. Nacilien was served by a trauma therapy designed for
children, and after a time he was asked what he wanted to be when he grew
up. Nacilien said he wanted to become the captain of a ship so he could bring
medical supplies to sick people. Like Nacilien, a recipient of help becomes
the provider of blessings for others. He is transformed and will look for every

opportunity to give to another in need (http://www.weekofcompassion.org/from-the-field/).

There are those who offer help, those who receive help, and then there are those who witness it. As observers, they too are blessed, transformed, and brought joy by witnessing the act of sharing. We witness others who give as an expression of their love for God's people, and we are moved to share too. We see joy resulting from someone sharing, and we are inspired to follow suit. We experience secondhand the awakening to faith gifted to another by blessed sharing, and we feel a tug from God. We are called to share, to bless, to transform, and to bring joy.

If we are the ones giving, the ones receiving, or the ones watching it all transpire, we find the act of sharing has a multiplying affect. Sharing overflows with many thanks to God and exposes one to a life overflowing with new opportunities to share.

14

THANK GOD!

What good comes from thanking God? In so doing, do we negate the good works of actively involved humans? Are there not many of life's gifts that we are actually due? Much of it we've earned, haven't we? If thanks is just something given away and not intentionally lived, then our gratitude may not be fully known by another. In choosing to thank God, we acknowledge a greater picture and choose to accept the part we play in continuing a stream of blessings.

ALL THE THANKS IS FOR GOD

"Riches and honor come from You, and You rule over all. In your hand are power and might; and it is in your hand to make great and to give strength to all. And now, our God, we give thanks to You and praise your glorious name." I Chronicles 29:1–20

Out of love for his Lord, King David wanted to build a temple for God and the Ark of the Covenant (I Chronicles 28:2). Instead, it was his son, Solomon, that God chose to build the temple (I Chronicles 28:6). The Israelites sacrificed their wealth, their talents, and their time to the construction of the Lord's temple. Throughout I and II Chronicles, the efforts of the people and their kings are described, and the wealth dedicated to this act of faith is chronicled. And yet, in all the verses, not once is a word of thanks spoken to the ones who built the temple; the ones who donated the gold, silver, and building supplies; or the ones who designed and oversaw the efforts. Thanks is not even expressed for Kings David or Solomon. Only one character receives any thanks—the Lord God is thanked.

In the passage recounting King David's last words to the Israelites, he explains that any gift we offer to God is a gift originally given to us by God (verses 12, 14b, and 16). This is a stark contrast to the modern cultural understanding of our wealth as something we have personally earned by our wisdom, talent, and effort. Perhaps this contemporary concept makes it harder to part with one's gold today. And perhaps this same idea is what creates the hunger for recognition, and thanks in us. If I give you what is mine, I deserve thanks. Whereas, if what I am giving is first a gift to me, I don't crave the words of thanks as much. The giving is just the next logical step in passing along what is needed by oneself, and then others.

We can gain a fresh perspective on giving from this story in Chronicles. In giving freely to a cause greater than oneself, and doing so within one's community, a synergistic outcome can occur. And since the outcome is greater than any one person's efforts, the thanks goes beyond any one individual. Within a faith community, the gratitude and praise go to God.

I like to imagine a totally different scene where King David stands before the gathered crowds at the Emmy Awards. The envelope is opened, his name is announced as the award winner, and he walks to the podium and reads his prepared statement:

"I would like to thank all of those whose efforts will make this temple possible. To the goldsmiths, I thank you for your world-renowned craftsmanship that will fashion the donated materials into the most glorious designs. And of course, a great thanks goes out to the family of the Nebulun who gave so generously of their silver collection and the Rueben family for the iron. I want to be sure to recognize the people of Tyre, who will provide the cedar for all the wooden needs of this grand temple, as well as the fabric of exquisite colors. And my thanks would not be complete without recognizing the family of Levi, without whom the temple needs would never be fully met. And all the little people who gave a coin here, a prayer there, let this be my thanks that you too have had a part in this award I receive today. Thank you all for recognizing my effort in building a lasting emblem of gratitude to our Lord, the one true God. Thank you."

As the King returns to his seat, members of the tribes of Asher and Gad fume that their contributions are not publicly recognized. The tribes of Simeon and Dan stand and walk out in disgust for their efforts have also gone unnoticed. The army commanders sit, quietly hiding their disappointment although internally they realize that once again their life-threatening duties are apparently viewed as expected behavior and not as a saving grace for the Israelites. Without the safety their forces provide, there would be no wealth, no security while building the temple.

Fortunately, this was not the scene recorded or lived during the end of King David's reign. Rather, the only gratitude expressed then was, "Thanks be to God." Everyone gathered understood that God, the Creator of Heaven and Earth, the ultimate Ruler of Israel, established their place in that ancient world.

To be honest, though, I often long for recognition of my efforts within the faith community in the form of some expression of thanks. Unlike King David, I sometimes fail to notice my God's role in the success of ministry efforts. I overlook that my talents have been developed by God and cultivated by God's servants. In ministry, talented, faithful servants surround me, and their efforts elevate and bring to life what I only dream of individually. And others who share their faith and inspire me, help to cultivate what I call my dreams. Without the company of the faithful, no effort of my own will build a temple or a program. Alone, I cannot raise a child of faith or inspire a cause. I don't do any of it alone. Then why do I expect the glory of being raised up and singled out for thanks?

If ultimately, God is the only one worthy of thanks, why do we bother saying thanks to anyone else? If the Christmas gift from my brother was purchased with assets he was able to earn only because of God's gifts to my brother, which empower his success at work, why should I thank my brother? If Habitat for Humanity only functions by God's grace, why feel any gratitude toward that organization for my new home? If your abundance allowed you to share food with me, but you are only enjoying such abundance by God's providence, why should I thank you? **Well**, I still say, give, and live my thanks because in their state of generosity, all those people have chosen to share their abundance with me. So, thank you very much! I appreciate your gifts. And I will live my thanks to my God, too. Thank you, God, for the gifts you share with others, who in turn share with me.

Out of love for God, King David gave, and the Israelites gave, and their willingness to do so was chronicled in chapter 29, verse 9: "Then the people rejoiced because these had given willingly." They knew the choice was theirs alone: the choice to give back to God what God gave to them, or to hang on to their wealth and deny the part God played in their good fortunes. But they gave, and they rejoiced in doing so. This is thankful living!

THANK GOODNESS

Why do we bother saying thanks to God? What good comes of it? Does God really care or want our verbal thanks? An article by Daniel C. Dennett entitled "Thank Goodness" suggests that such activity is worthless. His work is published as a collection in Christopher Hitchens' book, *Portable Atheist*. In this book, the famed atheist rails on those of us who choose to thank God rather than thank goodness. Dennett expresses his frustration with those who do nothing but say thanks to God in prayer rather than do good in the world:

"Or you could thank God—but the very idea of repaying God is ludicrous. What could an omniscient, omnipotent Being (the Man Who has Everything?) do with paltry repayments from you? ... the idea that by thanking God you are actually doing some good has got to be understood to be just symbolic, too. I prefer real good to symbolic good."

Unlike Dennett, I still see significant good resulting from thanking God. And yet, I do agree with Dennett that words alone are insufficient. Thank you is something meant to be lived. Without living our thanks, the words become shallow and sarcastic. Perhaps a few examples will clarify my point:

Sometimes my family thanks me for preparing dinner and then leaves the table quickly to watch TV without offering to help clean up. I feel like those words of thanks are offered as an apology for not wanting to contribute to the hard work of creating a family meal, but wanting to benefit from it. Saying thanks is easier than doing thanks.

When coordinating youth events for our church, there are a few adults who stand back and say, "thank you for working with the kids," but never offer support for these programs or young people. Not all adults have the gifts needed to lead teens, and yet these adults could try to learn their names, say hello, and support their program and funding efforts. Just saying thanks requires much less effort.

Occasionally at the checkout, a sales clerk will ring up my order, hand me my change, and thank me for shopping at her store without ever looking at me. The clerk who looks up and smiles at me is the one who lives her thanks.

Imagine thanks being expressed more like this:

Our church's youth thanked the family that organized monthly food collections for the local pantry. Each month, after the worship service when the food is collected, those same youth carry the collected food to the organizer's van.

Late one evening, having forgotten that her uniform needed to be washed for the next day's game, my daughter thanked me for doing her wash that night. The next day, she washed her own uniform along with a load for the family.

In a distant city, neighbors care for the widower living down the street. His adult children are sure to thank the kindhearted neighbors whenever visiting their dad. And back in their own city, they visit an elderly lady that lives near them. They are living their thanks.

I can thank God for the beautiful forest that surrounds our home, and then plant a tree in a nearby park. I can thank God for health, and then, while subbing in the school cafeteria, I make time to talk with children about eating healthy foods. I can thank God for a good book, and then make a contribution to my local library.

It is sad to think there are some who think that Christians' prayers and worship are wasted time. I don't blame them, though. I see it as a call for me to live out my silent thanks, being sure to live as thankfully as I feel. Rather than placing judgment on the atheist, his critical words summon me to act more lovingly, more kindly, more generously, and more thankfully.

In this same article, Daniel Dennett calls his readers to thank all the good folks who bring about our blessings rather than thanking a nonexistent celestial being. As I see it, he has a valid point. Much of the good I experience daily is due to the good will of many unnamed people. I drive on a smooth road, paved and designed by strangers. I use a computer engineered by people I'll never meet (but maintained by the amazing Chris Cobb). My teeth are straight, clean, and healthy due to my dentist and an orthodontist I haven't seen in 35 years. And people, many whom I will never even know by name, settled this little corner of Ohio, a place that makes me so happy! I thank the good work, good intentions, and good heartedness of all those people. Thank goodness!

Yet, there is more to our blessed state than can be credited to any human goodness. For instance, as I ran this morning, the sun cast a warm, golden shine on the earth, and I don't know what person to thank for that. A very dear friend of ours is opening his life and heart to our family and what's happening is more than human friendship. The leaves transform from a singular shade of green into a multiplicity of eye-catching color. Although it looks as if an artist has loosed her pallet of paint on the canvas of trees, no person created this scene. I have wealth I didn't earn, health I am only partially responsible for, a loving family I never chose, and intelligence that I cannot even fully use. I am loved despite my faults and forgiven despite my continued failings. Thank God!

Not all goodness can be credited to human effort. It's God's doing. And some of the goodness that can be credited to human effort, upon closer examination, is found to be motivated and inspired by human faithfulness. In other words, God inspires us to create, build, heal, help, design, establish, care, and do our best out of love for Him. Where Dennett writes, "Good intentions and inspiration are simply not enough," I ask, where else does one start? We start with faithful inspiration and God-directed intentions and go out to make the world a better place. I dream of creating a heaven-like place right here and now. I will try to fill the world with God's goodness for I am inspired by faith in God.

We respond to God's grace with a desire to continue the goodness. We respond to the benevolence of others with thankfulness and more good works. In talking about this idea of goodness with three different friends, I found how their unique perspectives reflected the idea of responding to God by living thanks. Elizabeth described thankful expressions as a "sweet human effort of acting in kind." Bonnie needs to ask for help in some situations due to her physical disabilities. She recently asked a new friend for help at a picnic. She did help and then actually thanked Bonnie for asking for help. Bonnie felt the "true sincerity" of that woman's thanks because of the actions that accompanied the words. Add to that, a work story from Ann. When customers call in with troubles and ask for assistance, Ann always completes the call with, "Thank you for calling." She says she doesn't feel as if she has lived up to her words, "thank you," until she has done her very best to help those customers even after the phone call has ended. In all three cases, my friends have seen God's love expressed through thankful living or have been the one's living thankfully. God has been actively involved is their living thanks or seeing cause for thanks.

In my world, it's more than goodness that makes the world wonderful, it's God in our midst. Thanks be to God.

BLESSING OR ENTITLEMENT?

"It is good to give thanks to the Lord, to sing praises to your name, O Most High." Psalms 92:1–4

The colors of this morning's sunrise are nothing I earned. A friend's faithfulness is not owed to me. My health is due only in part to my healthy lifestyle choices. I didn't plant the flowers I enjoyed today. And even if I did, I cannot take sole credit for their blossoming beauty. The rain refreshes the deserving and the undeserving. There are days when I don't merit my daughter's love. My wealth is due only in part to my hard work. It is also due to where, when, and to whom I was born. The birdsong I delight in was not sung for me.

Daily, the blessings I encounter are countless. How I choose to view those blessings is up to me. Do I merit all this good? Did I have it coming? Is it all earned? **Or**, do I choose to acknowledge that much of my life's joy is like a gift: given, not earned?

I choose to give thanks for these as blessings, gifts, and thankworthy experiences. None of this is fully earned, wholly owned, completely deserved, or entirely warranted. Each joy-giving element of my life deserves recognition and thanks. And so, I say thanks! Thanks for the flowers, the sunrise, the rain, and the song. Thanks for the love of friends and family. Thanks for my health, my wealth, and my employment.

If I choose to see these things as my privilege, my right, my property, as mine, I lose a source of joyous gratitude. And if they are taken away, I feel more than sadness. I feel cheated. I feel robbed. Their memory then evokes rage for an injustice inflicted upon me rather than gratitude for a recalled happiness.

Counting our blessings and feeling the joy of thanks compels us to rethink our place in the world, not as ones who are utterly deserving, but rather, as ones grateful for what we have. We can choose to see ourselves as blessed or as entitled. The former elicits thanks. The latter does not.

And I think it is good to give thanks to our God! In fact, I think it is good to **live** thanks to our God!

15

VEILED CAUSE FOR THANKS

Gratitude will not always manifest itself in song and dance. It may not even foster a smile. However, the assurance that in all of life's circumstances there lies reasons for thankfulness may be what sustains us through the worst.

WHEN JOY IS HARD TO FIND

"Rejoice always, pray without ceasing, give thanks in all circumstances; for this is the will of God in Christ for you." I Thessalonians 5:16–18

Pete is a struggling friend of mine. The weekend his little brother, Kenny, was placed in hospice care, Pete was heartbroken. "Life isn't fair," he told me numerous times. Joyful thanksgiving was the furthest thing from his mind at that time.

All this talk about thankfulness and joyous living can seem pretty shallow when there is genuine cause for sadness, disappointment, or anger. Where does thankfulness fit in under the worst circumstances? When life isn't fair, how are we supposed to give thanks? What on earth was Paul talking about when he told the Thessalonians to give thanks in all circumstances? And just what is there to be thankful for when your little brother is going to die?

No one is spared life's sadness. Some experience much more sadness than others. And Pete is absolutely right—life is not fair. Each individual does not receive an equal share of wealth, health, family support, and love. So, can we be thankful for what we have when we know others have more good stuff and less of the sad and bad stuff?

Perhaps life is not about comparing life situations. Perhaps thankful living comes from not missing out on any little thing worthy of our gratitude. Kenny is dying, but he does have family support. Kenny is dying, but the hospice care is a godsend. Kenny is dying, but Pete is remembering with his brother many of the joys they have shared in life.

Maybe there are times when finding cause for thanksgiving is like an Easter egg hunt in the snow. We know there must be treats there hiding for us, but it just seems as though looking for them takes too much energy and that its not right to have to look for them in such trying circumstances.

And sometimes thankfulness doesn't make us dance with joy. Sometimes thankfulness is just enough to keep us persevering. Recognizing any small cause for gratitude gives us the next breath and we continue to **exist with purpose.**

And what about the rest of verse 18, "… for this is the will of God in Christ Jesus for you"? Does Paul mean to say that God intentionally places us into every circumstance we find ourselves in? Or is it that it's God's will for us to find cause for thanksgiving wherever we find ourselves? I believe God created us with the hope that we could find purpose and thanksgiving in all our circumstances. I am not of the mind that God places us in trying situations to see if we can "pass the test." But I do believe that God has given us the tools necessary to withstand the trying times. God's will is that we find cause for rejoicing and faith enough to continue to pray. God believes we will detect a genuine occasion for gratitude. In doing so, we might just find cause for thanks that will give us reason to **exist with purpose**, even when joy is hard to find.

MY "PERSECUTION"

"For this is thankworthy/For it is a credit to you—if being aware of God you endure pain while suffering unjustly." I Peter 2:19 (KJV/NRSV)

In the fall of my junior high years, I faced a recurring dilemma every Friday night. The neighborhood kids would all gather after dark and play football, while elsewhere at the same time, my church friends gathered in the youth room for an evening of fun and games. Those neighborhood kids were pretty cool and I really needed to improve my "cool" rating among their ranks. Hanging out with these kids seemed like a good way to make ins with them. Since our house had a good "playing field" with just enough lighting and just enough grass, they liked to play in my very own front yard. During the games, while blocking, tackling, and huddling, girls and boys had a kind of "safe" time to touch one another, even if just rubbing shoulders or tackling with a bear hug. It was the kind of junior high playfulness that our young hormones craved.

On those Fridays, the kids would start to gather on the sidewalk corner by my house and I would be visiting with the cute guys and the cool girls. The church fun night starting time would approach just as I was groovin' with the neighborhood gang. If on such a night I told the neighborhood kids I had to go to church, the football game couldn't be held in my yard. As some boys would start to complain, one of the girls would say, "Oh yeah, Pam's born again and she's gotta go to church tonight." That comment would raise questions, "What do you mean she's born again?" and I would have to explain, again, in front of my peers—those really cool kids—what my faith meant to me and why I chose to follow Jesus. Explain in my own words… every time… standing in the dark yard… wanting to play football… walking away from a fun time with the "in crowd"… the group that I wasn't really a part of… where I just stood on the sidelines and shared my front yard.

See, some of those girls knew that I was a "born again Christian." In my bedroom, on the bulletin board, they had seen the special pamphlet I received in the spring from the Christian rally held in our church fellowship hall. The blue book with a white dove and words "born again" caught their eye, and I found myself explaining what it all meant to me. I told these girls that I walked to the front of the stage that day and committed myself to Jesus Christ. Being "born again" meant that I loved Jesus and He was my first choice in everything. On those Fridays I found myself confessing this to a whole crowd of frisky 13- and 14-year-olds. That was my persecution.

Some nights it was embarrassing for me, but it wasn't really much of a persecution, was it? And it's not really now either. But that's the closest encounter with unjust suffering I can come up with when I try to relate to the words of this scripture—of enduring pain while being aware of and choosing God.

Honestly, I can't remember a time when I felt like I suffered for my faith. There were times growing up that my faith made me stand out from my friends, but it wasn't a cause of suffering. As a young adult, there were times when people chose to avoid me because of my faith and how I chose to express that in my vocation. Again, I didn't suffer because of it even if I did miss out on some adult activities, like being invited to party all night long or being the object of a man's attention for one night. As a parent, our family chose not to participate in local soccer leagues because the games and practices were held on Sundays, but also because we don't care for soccer. So again, no suffering resulted.

The author of I Peter wrote to encourage those who suffer unjustly. In this verse, "it is a credit to you" could also be translated as "this is thankworthy," with the intention of encouraging those whose faith causes persecution and suffering. I think suffering here means a great deal more than missing a football game, a party, or a soccer season. But still, when I was 13 and I showed up at church on those Friday nights, there were folks who saw my actions as thankworthy and told me in their own way. First, my youth pastor, Gil Hubbard—who drove three hours from seminary to start his weekend with us playing foosball, guitar, and checkers—greeted me with his contagious smile and warm eyes and literally said thanks for coming tonight. Second, I felt the thank you gestured by the parents who would chaperone and allow us to run around the church rooms and corridors in ways that other church members would have been appalled to see. Third, my own mom, who kept her Friday evening schedule flexible enough that I could decide last minute if I was going to stay home and play football or ask for a ride to church for our fun night. She never once complained or pressured me to choose one way or another, and in so doing, expressed her thanks for who I was, an awkward teenage girl.

I'm not sure what I craved more in those odd teenage years, the physical contact of the neighborhood football games or the affirmation of Christian fellowship. I'm not even sure I realized at the time how supportive the church adults were of me and my friends and our choices to come to church. But somehow, as I started to become aware of God's presence and chose to be with others who sought God, those leaders found a way to feed my craving for affirmation. They found my choices to be thankworthy and they expressed their thanks. And for my part, I continued to choose God-time even when that was a bit awkward.

There is the possibility that as of yet I've not been fully aware of God's need for me in this world. Perhaps there are no thanks due, for no real suffering has come my way. Maybe I have chosen the simple way. Maybe I have no right thinking this scripture could relate to me. Maybe. This is tough bread to swallow, hard words to hear.

Maybe I am the one called to live my thanks for those who **have** made the hard choices. Those who **have** placed themselves in harm's way to stay true to their faith deserve words and actions of love, support, and thanks from people like me.

Where do we find ourselves?

A KICK IN THE TEETH

"But love your enemies, do good, and lend expecting nothing in return."
Luke 6:32–38

Expect no thanks, no credit, no reward, no pat on the back for loving those who are easy to love, for lending to those you know will pay back, or for doing good to those you know will be good to you. The Gospel lesson is clear, even if the various translations vary somewhat.

As Jesus spoke to His followers, He set the bar high. The message wasn't easy to hear. Love the unloving. Lend to the ungrateful. Be good to the wicked. There aren't too many days that I set out to do what Jesus taught here, and I'm afraid if I did I might just get kicked in the teeth—or worse!

But maybe, just maybe, Jesus knew just what he was talking about. There have been times in my life when a person I thought was unlovable was only unloved. Sometimes an act of loving care can bring out the best in someone, the side she never had reason to show. And there have been times when I've been kicked in the teeth. Let me tell you about one of each.

First, here's a "kicked in the teeth" story: While serving in a nice suburban church, a stranger came up to me in the church parking lot asking for assistance. He and his family needed lodging for the night while they waited for his brother to come with money for them to continue their trip south to his wife's family and his new job. I put them up in a local motel, bought the family a pizza, and made plans to meet them in the morning to send them on their way after being repaid. The next morning, I arrived with muffins for everyone only to find the motel room vacant. They skipped town. As a young woman with very little savings, I was left with a large debt to pay and a sad story to share. I never heard from those folks again and certainly never received a thank you.

Here's a story about bringing out the best in another by showing love: Leonard was a young adult, a loner in the community, a little rough around the edges, and in painter's garb when I met him on one of his infrequent visits to church. Weeks later, I needed my apartment painted and thought of the young painter. I found a way to contact him and hired him to paint. Looking for recommendations from church friends, everyone simply said Leonard was really quiet and no one knew about his professional abilities. His estimate was high and I wondered if he was getting the best of me. But, I gave him a chance. It took him quite a while to do the work and we had some time to talk—well, I talked to him. He mostly smiled and nodded occasionally. I talked about the church and my friends there and I invited him to come more often. He just painted, and his work was perfect, utterly polished. After, he began to attend church regularly. The young adults of the church took him under their wings. Leonard was still quiet, but felt trusted by this community. He blossomed. He found ways to live his thanks, because he wasn't very good at saying it. He began to help the congregation and even donated his painting skills to the church. Leonard only needed to be loved. And I smiled, all my teeth fully intact.

Maybe that's a part of Jesus lesson: Take a chance. Be nice when its hard to be nice simply because that's when **nice** is most needed. I recovered from the motel lie and bruised ego, and went on to take chances with people again. Maybe because I'm naïve, maybe because I want to believe there's potential good in everyone, maybe because I just can't say no, but regardless, I generally find that Jesus' lesson is a good one for life. Love the unlovable.

However, the following is an important disclaimer: I don't always get it right and way too often I reject the unlovable, unlikable, or unkind. I guard my money, my ego, my time and don't give when its gonna be hard. I just wanted to make that clear. Because the previous story may have made it sound like I'm always getting it right. I don't. I just want to. So I write this as encouragement for you (I hope) and for me.

A FAITHFUL THANK YOU

"To You, O God of my ancestors, I give thanks and praise, for You have giv-

en me wisdom and power, and have revealed to me what we asked of You,
for You have revealed to us what the king ordered." Daniel 2:23

Once again, the scriptures tell us a story of inspirational faith when one of God's messengers gives thanks to God simply on faith that his prayers will be answered. This is another "please and thank you" story. Daniel is the inspirational character, Babylon is the setting, and mercy is the subject of his prayers.

The magicians and enchanters of the day were asked not only to interpret the King's dream, but also to tell the King just what it was he dreamed. The King wanted to dissuade any false interpretations and have these magical men prove their talents. Death awaited them if they failed and not one of them dared to guess what the King was dreaming. When Daniel, an exile among the Babylonians, heard of his fate, he rallied the prayer power of his fellow exiles and, lo and behold, the dream and the interpretation—not a particularly encouraging one for Babylon—was revealed to Daniel.

Then come the amazing words of thanks. Before he takes the dream's bad news to the King, he thanks God for revealing the dream, it's meaning, and the expected mercy Daniel and the others hope for.

But wait just one minute here! First, how does Daniel know that this dream of his is actually the King's dream? Next, what makes Daniel so sure that he has interpreted the dream properly? And most pressing, why does Daniel think that this King is going to believe the interpretation that Daniel is offering, especially since Daniel will be prophesying the downfall of the Babylonian empire?

Daniel's prayer of thanks and praise seems a bit premature at this point. When I have proof that my prayers have been answered, then I breathe a sigh of relief and say a prayer of thanks. In other words, if I were Daniel I would be thanking God after my audience with the King, after he had lifted the death decree, after my friends and I were out of the woods.

When Daniel gives thanks to God, he also gives a lesson to the doubting "faithful" about God's faithfulness. If he asked God for the dream, God must have delivered it. If he asked God for the interpretation, God must have provided it. If he asked God for mercy, being spared death at the King's hand, God must have arranged it. This is a faith so ingrained in Daniel's being that he is assured of God's trustworthiness.

My children head out the door and down the street to get on the bus, and

I never doubt for one second that they will board the bus and be at school all day. I have counted on my husband's faithfulness for 20 years and never once have I doubted it. I rely upon my fellow committee members to attend the meetings. I count on my parents' enduring love. I expect the oncoming driver to stay on their side of the road. Daniel has the same faithful expectations of his God and he bases his very existence upon them.

If we are able to trust flawed humans to maintain their faithfulness, how can we doubt our perfect God? Somehow, we do. Perhaps this story will give us the courage of Daniel to expect God to be faithful to us. Maybe we can also say a "please and thank you" prayer.

It's nearly midnight and my 16-year-old son is due home any minute now. I want the faith of Daniel that can offer up one of those please and thank you prayers. God, please help Andy arrive home safely and thank you, God, for getting Andy home safely. Such a faith would calm my pounding heart and allow me to sleep rather than sit here typing away with jittery pecks at the keyboard. Such a faith would place the whole situation in God's hands, believing that God is with me and Andy whatever we must face. Living such a confident faith would propel me from fright to might, ready to move on to do the real work of the day and not the worry of the night.

Daniel's example can be a tough one to internalize, but it's a good one to return to repeatedly. Each time I read this story, I remember where I want my faith to be. So I'll keep practicing those prayers. Please God... thank you God...

PART 4
BIBLE STUDY GUIDE

AN OUTLINE FOR A FOUR-SESSION BIBLE STUDY

The following is a leader's guide that can be used for a small group study on the transformative power of thankfulness. It is designed for four 90-minute sessions, although it can easily be reformatted for more weeks, with greater discussion time or shorter sessions with less group participation. The participants will benefit from the study even if they have not read the book. Page references are offered to assist with leadership efforts.

SESSION ONE: INTRODUCTION AND EXPLORING SEE IT!

INTRODUCTION

Start with a discussion on thanks. Use the following to initiate conversation:

- **When** do we most regularly use thanks?

A few examples: Say it in response to niceties. Write it on notes. Respond to societal expectations. Use it for evening meal prayers. Teach children to respond with please and thank you.

- **Tell a story** of a time when you expressed thanks or received thanks.

- **Share a scripture** that you remember in part or whole that speaks about thanks.

Explain the three parts of thankfulness covered in this book: See it! Say it! Live it! (summarized below).

See it! If we were more aware of everything that could elicit our thanks, we would be more content with what we have. We might need less, we might be happier. We might be better able to give/share.

Say it! When we say our thanks, we share our joy. We acknowledge another's worth. We give credit where credit is due. We have the power to transform others. We acknowledge our reliance on others, including God.

Live it! Thankful people live beyond themselves, better able to help, love, and care for God's creation.

This first week together, we'll look at Biblical stories whose characters **saw** cause for thanks. In each case, their thanks transformed others or themselves.

DISCUSSION

Choose a format for discussion. The group may read and discuss both passages together. Or, the large group can break out into two small groups, with each group reading and discussing only one scripture passage and then reporting their findings back to the large group.

John 6:11* Jesus gives thanks for an *interruption* of *insufficient* food, an offering that others saw as *insult*. Refer to pages 20–27, "Thanks for a Few Fish."

*Verses 1–14 tell the story.

- How can we alter our perspectives so that we may also find reasons for thanks through the interruptions of life? The insufficiencies? The insults? He saw reason for thanks for: what I have, who I am, and where I am in life.

Jonah 2:9* Refer to pages 51–52, "Thanks from the Belly of a Fish."

*Read the whole prayer (verses 1–9). Read Chapter 1 to see how Jonah found himself in the fish's belly.

- How can one possibly find cause for thanks after three days in the belly of a fish? I call it "fishbelly" time. It's like a time out, something we need when we're overlooking all we have to be thankful for.

- Are there intentional steps you can take to establish some "fish-belly" time when needed?

CLOSING

Summarize the discussion of scripture stories. Invite participants to reread the scriptures during the week and focus on **seeing** cause for thanks.

Close in a prayer where all participants offer God thanks for something they have recently seen as thankworthy.

SESSION TWO: SAY IT!

INTRODUCTION

As the group gathers, summarize the last session, being sure to mention the ideas of seeing thanks, saying thanks, and living thanks. In this session we will explore saying thanks. Start the discussion with the following questions:

- When do you **say** your thanks?

- When do you hear it and it sounds genuine? And when does it not?

DISCUSSION

We will look at three biblical accounts revealing characters that say their thanks: the Psalmist, Jesus, and Paul. Again, this discussion may take place as one large group or three smaller groups. Following each scripture passage listing, you will find suggested questions and comments for discussion.

Psalms 92:1* "It is good to give thanks to the Lord." This seems to be the most basic of thanks stories in the Bible. Refer to pages 69–79, "Thankful Expressions in the Psalms."

*As always, read the whole Psalm, at least through verse 4.

- What happens to a people who forget to say their thanks when they recover from a horrendous time?

Many Psalms use thanks and singing together.

Many recount the hardships followed by God's saving acts.

- In what ways do the Psalms call us to "give thanks"?

- To whom does the thanks go in most all scripture?

Also Psalms 95:1, 2; Psalms 100:4; Psalms107:1, 2a, 8, 15, 21, 22, 31, 32 (troubled times with relief from God); Psalms 111:1 (in the company of the upright); Psalms 118:1, 21, 29 (victorious song of thanks); Psalms 139:14 (knit); Psalms 147:7 (one verb for us, 20 for God).

John 11:41* Although in the Lord's Prayer there is no reference to thanks, "Hallowed be Thy name" may be a form of praise, which is kind of like thanks. However, in this story we hear Jesus say thanks to God, finally. Refer to pages 60–61, "For Having Heard Me."

*Read the whole chapter to familiarize yourself with the story of Lazarus' illness and death, as well as the crowd's response.

- Why would Jesus weep and then six verses later say his thanks?

- And what's with praying aloud? He knew that His verbal prayer of thanks would endanger his life. Did He want His thanks to be a **witness** to others?

- And why say thanks **before** the outcome is known? I call this a "please and thank you" prayer. Again, an example of Jesus' living totally on faith.

Paul's Openings in his Letters: Many of the Epistles open with words of thanks for the letters' recipients.

"First, I thank my God through Jesus Christ for all of you, because your faith is proclaimed throughout the world." Romans 1:8

"I give thanks to my God always for you because of the grace of God that has been given to you in Christ Jesus." I Corinthians 1:4

"...for in every way you have been enriched in Christ, in speech and

knowledge of every kind." I Corinthians 1:5

"I thank my God every time I remember you, constantly praying with joy in every one of my prayers for all of you, because of your sharing in the gospel from the first day until now." Philippians1:3–5

"In our prayers for you we always thank God, the Father of our Lord Jesus Christ, for we have heard of your faith in Christ Jesus and of the love that you have for all the saints, because of the hope laid up for you in heaven." Colossians 1:3–5

"We always give thanks to God for all of you and mention you in our prayers, constantly remembering before our God your work of faith and labor of love and steadfast hope in Jesus Christ." I Thessalonians 1:2–3

"We must always give thanks to God for you, brothers and sisters, as is right, because your faith is growing abundantly…" II Thessalonians1:3a

"… and the love of everyone of you for one another is increasing." II Thessalonians1:3b

"I am grateful to God… when I remember you constantly in my prayers night and day." II Timothy 1:3

"When I remember you in my prayers, I always thank my God because I hear of your love for all the saints and your faith toward Jesus." Philemon 4 and 5

"Paul's" letters* Paul says thanks for people at the start of his letters. Even when he wrote to admonish them, he started with thanks for something about them. Like a loving parent, he states his love for the child and dislike for the action. Say "thank you for you" first.

*We will not discuss at this time the actual authors of each of these letters.

- What were some specifics for which Paul was thankful?

- If we too started with thanks for others, how could this impact our interactions with people?

- If we chose to be like Paul, how might that be reflected in our actions and conversations with those we know and love? With strangers?

CLOSING

Summarize the discussion at the close. Ask for the participants to share a word of thanks in a closing prayer circle. If folks are comfortable doing so, each could give thanks to God for the one standing to their left.

For folks to take home: Include a Psalm of thanks in each of your days this week. Read the entire Psalm, with attention given to the verses listed:

Psalms 95:1, 2

Psalms 100:4

Psalms107:1, 2a, 8, 15, 21, 22, 31, 32

Psalms 111:1

Psalms 118:1, 21, 29

Psalms 139:14

Psalms 147:7

SESSION THREE: LIVE IT!

INTRODUCTION

This third week together we'll see what happens when one lives a life that is full of thanks! More than seeing or saying thanks, what happens when we live our thanks? It's the **pay-it-forward** concept. I can tell you "thank you" or I can live my thanks to you by being a blessing to another in need.

- Have you had an experience when someone says thanks but their actions do not?

Examples: walk away from the dinner table, but leave a mess for the cook to clean; return a borrowed item in disrepair; show up late with no explanation

- How about the opposite experience when someone has forgotten to say thanks but you know they are grateful?

Examples: a child needs help getting started but gets homework done; parents who once played with their younger children find them growing up and now helping younger kids in the neighborhood

DISCUSSION

These three scriptures explore ways of living one's thankfulness. In one large group or three small groups, read and discuss the verses.

II Corinthians 9:11–15* Refer to pages 122–123, "Thanks is Good Medicine."

*Or the entire chapter

- In verse 15, what is the gift?

- Who is inspired by the giving? (The giver, the receiver, the observer, God?)

- From whence comes the abundance? God gives more? The giver senses she has more to give?

Our giving thanks can encourage others, even convert them into giving people. When we are aware of and thankful for what we have, we share. When we share, others give thanks. They may also become aware of what they have—what they can share. And still others, just watching, give thanks and may share.

Daniel 2:23* Daniel thanks God for something he's not even sure will work yet. Another "please and thank you" prayer, and an example of what living with thanks may look like. Refer to pages 137–139, "A Faithful Thank You."

*Read or tell the story of the entire chapter.

- What did Daniel have to be thankful for? He'd been plucked from his home, a part of the royalty of Jerusalem, and now found himself in the midst of page training, as an exile.

- How did he know he had anything to be thankful for? How did he know this was the right dream or the right interpretation?

- Have you ever had a sense so strong in your faith life?

- What effect does living thankfully have on our understanding of our daily occurrences?

Matthew 26:26–27* Jesus lives His thanks for God, and for us, by saying thanks for the cup of His own blood. Refer to pages 104–106, "A Living

Prayer."

Mark 14:23, Luke 22:19–20, I Corinthians 11:23

- What is Jesus thanking God for in this verse?

- How is thanks here like our prayers at mealtime? How is it different?

- Compare verse 27 to 39. How does the first impact the second? (Is it possible that having first recognized His thanks for an opportunity, He had courage to pursue His call, as frightening as it may have been?

- What's going on here theologically? What do these passages teach us about Jesus? About us? About how the two interact?

CLOSING

Summarize the lesson's discussion and close in prayer, either the Lord's Prayer or a group prayer.

SESSION FOUR: THANKFUL PEOPLE & PUTTING THE YOU IN THANK YOU

INTRODUCTION

As the study closes this week, we'll determine ways to ensure that thankfulness infuses our daily living. Start with the thoughts inspired by this Jewish morning prayer, introduced to me by my pastor, Chad Delaney:

> *"Modeh ani lifanecha melech chai v'kayam shehechezarta bi nishmahti b'chemlah, rabah emunatecha."*

> *"I offer thanks before you, living and eternal King, for you have mercifully restored my soul within me; Your faithfulness is great."*

This prayer is called the Modeh Ani and is the Hebrew Morning Prayer. The idea is that the first thing a Jewish person should do after opening their eyes in the morning is say the Modeh Ani—preferably in Hebrew, but English is okay, too. It's a good way for all of us to start our days.

The thanks offered God here are not for any tangible thing, anyone, or any part of creation. Thanks is simply for God's mercy.

- In what ways is this like the prayers of thanks you find yourself offering? How is this different than praising God, or is it? Do you give thanks for the non-tangible? What is God's mercy?

It is not always easy to identify the benefactor, the one who deserves our gratitude. Sometimes recognizing the **you** of thank you is where we have to start.

- Offer examples of thankful experiences when the "you" is unusual or hard to identify. For instance, whom do we thank for a park, a sunny day, a return to health, a good seat? Sometimes we have to dig for a benefactor. Sometimes it's just fate—or God! Even when the source is hard to find, being, saying, and living thanks is vital.

DISCUSSION

I Chronicles 16:1–4 and I Chronicles 23:30, 31 A Vocation of thanks! A big part of the job of several families of the Levi Tribe was simply to give thanks, either by praise or with instruments.

- In today's world, who are the ones with a vocation of thanks? Is there any such thing? If not a paid position, who are the people who give thanks or live thanks ceaselessly? Could that be OUR job?

Luke 17:11–19, Recognizing the source of the gift. Refer to pages 95–97, "Thanks from a Foreigner." Jesus heals a group. One says thanks to the **you**—to Jesus.

- Why this particular man? Is it possible that he, of all those who were sick, didn't expect to be healed?

- How full of gratitude was he? Have you ever felt so thankful to the "you" that you fell to your knees?

Verse 19: "Rise and go. Your faith has made you well." I thought Jesus made him well. I thought he was already healed.

- What could this statement mean?

ACTING OUT OUR THANKS:
SUGGESTIONS OF DAILY WAYS OF THANKS-LIVING

At this point begin a discussion about ways the participants may change their daily behavior in order to intentionally include thankfulness. See the suggestions below and a few resources that may be helpful:

Ways to See it!

- Start a thank you notebook and add daily entries.

- Start a thanks ritual that calls you to see thanks. For instance, put notes in a bowl of previously thought of thanks and be reminded of those good things. Or, when you take a handful of popcorn, M&M's, or grapes, think of one thing to be thankful for for each individual treat.

- Infuse repetitive tasks with thanks. Say thanks for each lap run, each dish washed, each mile driven, etc.

- Visit network sites of thanks:

  Thanksometer.com
  GraceInSmallThings.com
  Gratitudelog.com

Ways to Say it!

- Start your own thank-you note ritual. (e.g., commit to say one thanks, give an online thanks, and write one thanks every week/month)

- Put songs of thanks on your mp3 and sing along

- Find a gratitude partner (Dr. Robert Emmons, PhD in his book *Thanks! How Practicing Gratitude Can Make You Happier*) and correspond your thanks regularly, because saying your thanks makes it more real to you.

- Make a list of all the people you could say thank you to: doctors, sales clerks, service reps, neighbors, school officials, safety forces, etc. After you have a nice, long list, start saying thanks to those folks.

Ways to Live it!

- If you choose to pledge to church, consciously make it an act of your thanks. Be aware of that every time you give.

- Play a game for a day where you count how many people you can get to say thank you to you for kind and thoughtful things you do. Although it's a silly game, learn from the experience and be mindful of how you can be a thankful blessing to others.

- Catch yourself being ungrateful. Find a way to transform your attitude.

- If we choose, we could say aloud what we plan to do to put our one-month study on thanks into action.

CLOSING

Participants may offer a prayer of thanks and also prayerfully ask God's help in their personal journeys towards thankful living.

www.ingramcontent.com/pod-product-compliance
Lightning Source LLC
Chambersburg PA
CBHW060252050426
42448CB00009B/1618

9 780998 550305